# STOP

# OVERTHINKING

Use Brainstorming and Stop Overthinking and
Decluttering

(The Practical Guide With the Most Effective
Strategies for Retrain Your Brain)

**Robert McGahan**

Published by Knowledge Icons

**Robert McGahan**

All Rights Reserved

ISBN 978-1-990084-63-8

Legal & Disclaimer

The information contained in this book is not designed to replace or take the place of any form of medicine or professional medical advice. The information in this book has been provided for educational and entertainment purposes only.

The information contained in this book has been compiled from sources deemed reliable, and it is accurate to the best of the Author's knowledge; however, the Author cannot guarantee its accuracy and validity and cannot be held liable for any errors or omissions. Changes are periodically made to this book. You must consult your doctor or get professional medical advice before using any of the suggested remedies, techniques, or information in this book.

Upon using the information contained in this book, you agree to hold harmless the Author from and against any damages, costs, and expenses, including any legal fees potentially resulting from the application of any of the information provided by this guide. This disclaimer applies to any damages or injury caused by the use and application, whether directly or indirectly, of any advice or information presented, whether for breach of contract, tort, negligence, personal injury, criminal intent, or under any other cause of action.

You agree to accept all risks of using the information presented inside this book. You need to consult a professional medical practitioner in order to ensure you are both able and healthy enough to participate in this program.

# Table of Contents

## Introduction

The following chapters will discuss the best ways you can get around the problems associated with overthinking and procrastinating in order to manage your time and energies a bit more wisely.

Overthinking is one of those things in life which may be causing you unpleasantness every time it creeps into your mind. In fact, it might even be limiting your abilities to make the most of your time and effort. Needless to say, overthinking is one of those things which may be holding you back.

Most people spend a lot of their time overthinking and failing to realize that they can utilize their time in a more effective way. There are many reasons for overthinking, but what people do not realize is that it is as dangerous as any fatal disease.

That is why this book has been written with every intent to help you focus on the important things in life; the things which you truly treasure such as spending time with your loved ones and dedicating time to your favorite activities.

Great care has been taken to produce a book which has been useful and informative. Please take the time to focus on each of the chapters as they are filled with nuggets that will surely give you insights you can apply to your everyday life.

There are plenty of books on this subject on the market, thanks again for choosing this one! Every effort was made to ensure it is full of as much useful information as possible, please enjoy!

# Chapter 1: What Is Overthinking?

Why Do We Overthink?

So far, there are two major explanations for the reason people overthink:

The overthinking brain and

Contemporary culture.

The Overthinking Brain

Our brain is designed in such a way that all our thoughts are interconnected in networks and nodes. For instance, thoughts about work may be in one network, and thoughts about family in another.

There is a strong connection between our emotions and moods. Activities or circumstances that stimulate negative feelings seem to be connected to one network, while those that induce happiness are linked to another network.

Although such interconnectedness of feeling and thought can help people to think more efficiently, it can also make people overthink.

In general, negative moods often activate negative thoughts and memories, even if such thoughts are unrelated. Overthinking while in a negative mood can fill the mind with lots of negative ideas and the more such a person overthinks, the easier it will be for his brain to induce negative associations.

According to research by brain experts, it has been discovered that damage (or miswiring) of certain areas of the brain can make one prone to depression and overthinking. Such areas include the amygdala and hippocampus, which are involved in learning and remembering, and the prefrontal cortex, which helps to regulate emotions. This knowledge partly explains why some individuals overthink more than others.

**The Overthinking Generation.** The reports from the studies conducted by the author showed that young ones, as well as middle-aged individuals, do overthink even more than the elderly ones (those above 65 years) do.

What can be responsible for this? There are 4 possible cultural trends that can be responsible:

**Entitlement obsession:** Many today have an overdeveloped sense of entitlement. They are entitled to be rich, successful, and happy and as such, no one can hinder them from getting what they deserve. Thus, most people worry because they aren't getting what they deserve, they try to find out what is holding them back. Such overthinking attitude has turned many into a ticking bomb, ready to explode at the slightest provocation.

**The vacuum of values:** Majority of people today, especially the youth, have questioned all the values their parents handed over to them such as religion, culture, and social norms. Therefore, such ones are left with only a few choices and without values, such a person will end up questioning each choice he makes and keep wondering if he made the right choice. (This too can lead overthinking).

**Belly button culture:** Modern culture and popular psychology often encourage people to be more expressive and to develop more self-awareness. However, most people often take this to the extreme, thereby becoming excessively self-absorbed, they overanalyze themselves and their feelings. Many people waste too much time "staring at their navels," brainstorming over the meaning of each emotional change.

**The compulsive need for quick fixes:** The 21st century is filled with people who tend to search for quick fixes, instead of taking time to gradually work things out. For instance, if someone is sad or troubled, he can resort to some quick way out such as drinking alcohol, shopping, taking prescription drugs, engaging in a new sport or hobby, or some other activities. In summary, quick fixes only provide a temporary solution (or even wrong solution).

Overthinking Symptoms

Having a well-defined list of overthinking symptoms can be quite helpful. In fact, awareness is your best defense, it will help you to know when you are in the danger zone, and failure to be on guard is very dangerous for your mental well-being.

Watching out for the following symptoms can help you carry out an overthinking disorder test. If you observe that you are experiencing the overthinking disorder, you may observe one or more of these following symptoms:

**When you can't sleep:** Try as hard as you may to get a decent rest, but your mind won't just turn off. Then agitation and worries set in.

**If you self-medicate:** Research on overthinking disorder has shown that those suffering from it often resort to food, alcohol, drugs, or any means of modulating feelings.

**You're usually tired:** Tiredness can be as a result of insomnia, or due to repeated thinking which drains the strength out of you.

**You want to be in control everything:** You attempt to plan all aspects of your life to the very last detail. But the truth is, there's a limit to what you can control.

**You obsess about failure:** The fear of failure has made you turn into a perfectionist and you often imagine how bad things will turn out if things don't work out well.

**You fear the future:** Rather than being thrilled by what the future holds, you're stuck in your thoughts.

**You doubt your own judgment:** You reconsider every decision you make from what you wear, to what you say, and how you relate with others.

**You get tension headaches:** You might experience chronic tension headaches as though a tight band is around your temples. In addition, you might also feel pain or stiffness around the neck region. All these are signs that you need a long rest.

If any of the above signs happen all too often, psychologists will say you're an over-thinker or a ruminator. According to psychologists, over-thinking can affect performance, cause anxiety, or even lead to depression.

## Chapter 2: What Exactly Is Worry And

## Anxiety?

I am sure that these terms- 'anxiety' and 'worry' are terms that we use in our everyday speech, but then I can bet that we didn't know that these words mean different things, although only slightly different. So maybe we should start with that. Well, worry is nothing out of the norm; it is just a normal reaction to a potential or full-blown danger. This means that worry could be about an incidence that has happened, or an incidence that we incline will happen. Now, here is the divergence point between both terms. While worry is for both an intending occurrence, and a past incident, anxiety is constrained to the feeling of fear or agitation for an intending danger. Both worry and anxiety are automatic body reactions which could be a fight-or-flight response, but one is more justified and tangible than the other.

For instance, Anxiety or worry could arise when you feel threatened, when you are under pressure to perform, or when there is a challenging situation that you are going through, or are about to experience. This could be an exam, a job interview, or your first date. Everyone feels anxious and worries over different things and at different times.

Note that worry is not in itself a bad thing. Well, unlike the way many people paint it. The problem with worry and anxiety arises when it becomes excessive. So this means that if stress is in moderation, then it cannot be categorized as a bad thing. In fact, a life with zero worries is not something to be proud of. It can help you to stay at alert, to stay focused, and it could push you to be more, and achieve more. But when anxiety gets too perpetual or overwhelming, it then begins to pose severe problems for your health, your mental well-being, your relationship with others, and even your everday life. Once anxiety becomes overboard, then it is safe to say that the bearer is tending towards the possibility of suffering from an anxiety disorder.

Now the topic of anxiety disorder is a whole different topic on its own and will be discussed in the next chapter, but before we move into the next chapter, I'll discuss some symptoms that usually point to excessive anxiety and even causes of worry.

Excessive anxiety can be accompanied by a variety of physical symptoms, and it manifests in different people according to their body type. But commonly, these symptoms are related to the heart, lungs, nervous, and the gastrointestinal systems in the body. The following are some symptoms, which if felt, should be paid attention to.

Stomach upset

Diarrhea

Stressful breathing patterns
Pseudo faint feel
Heart attack
While some causal factors are internal to the body, the following are some of the common external factors that can cause anxiety:
Stress at work
Stress from school
Strain in a personal relationship such as marriage or friendships
Financial burden
Pressure
Stress from an emotional trauma such as the death of a loved one, a natural disaster, victimization by crime, physical abuse or sexual abuse Stress from a serious medical illness
Side effects of a medication
Intoxication (being "high" on) with an illicit drug, such as cocaine or amphetamines
Withdrawal from an illegal drug, such as opiates (for example, heroin) or from

prescription drugs like Vicodin, benzodiazepines, or barbiturates
Symptoms of a medical illness

There is a long, and inexhaustible list of these causal factors. The above are only some of the external causal factors.

## Chapter 3: Where To Start?

Before we jump right into our first exercise based on learning to recognize the signs of anxiety you may encounter in your everyday routine let's do a short background survey. As we mentioned in the introduction this is an interactive book. Please get a notebook or pad, and a pen and keep handy at all times. Stash it in your briefcase or tote bag. You will be using it for notes and exercises.

Throughout this book completed examples of the exercises will accompany the text to help explain the exercise. We will be referring back to these exercises when building the final action plan. When you finish Exercise 1 from chapter 8, you should have actual answers. For this exercise, I am providing suggestions only, as prompts.

Please complete this Background Survey on yourself. Answering these questions is a way to ground you. Throughout this book, you will be digging into areas of yourself that you haven't dealt with in a while, if ever. So, with all the changes, questions, and memories, you uncover this survey will help you back to center when you start to build your action plan.

What do you wish to accomplish during the time you have remaining to consider your life satisfying and well-lived - a life of few or no regrets?

(Family, career, care for others, wealth, land ownership/stewardship?

If there were a secret passion in your life, what would it be?

(Sports, art, oration, politics, drama, writing?)

How is the most effective way to manage you? Give yourself some tips.

(Be direct, carrot/stick; give examples, suggestions, etc.)

What is missing in your life? What would make your life more fulfilling?

(Relationships (friend/love), education, income, direction, discipline, etc.)

What qualities are present in people who inspire you?

(Honesty, financial savvy, business acumen, education, strong wills patience)

What or who sets you back from achieving your goals? What makes you feel undeserving or not "good" enough? What is your trigger?

(Athletic prowess, body image, intellect, cleverness, lack of family)

As your own coach, when you seem to be straying from your goal by procrastinating or self-sabotage, what can you say or does that will help you return to your action plan?

(Forgive and get back in the saddle, do something entirely different and not on any schedule, go to a movie, run five miles, get on your bike)

Exercise is going to be part of your action plan. Do you have a regular exercise routine? Please list.

(Run, walk w/dogs, swim, dance, racketball, tennis, bowling, clogging, etc.)

Do you have a primary care physician? If not please try to find one, if at all possible.

(Yes, no, can't afford - need to ask for help)

Are there any medical issues of which the physician should be aware? Please list.

(Diabetes, blood pressure, bone spurs, etc.)

Education & Action

For our first exercise, we are going to learn to document our worries, the chatter running around in our head that is the cause of this overthinking. The following example seems like it has nothing to do with overthinking and worrying. Well, it doesn't. It's about how to get to the root of the matter. Breaking down the barriers or clutter that keeps us from seeing the real problem.

There is a sales technique called **overcoming objections** that are taught to anyone needing to close a deal. From computer salesmen to petition gatherers. The idea is to drill down to find the real reason someone doesn't want to buy a system, try some new product, or sign a petition.

Let's say your company uses system ABC for its manufacturing plant. It gets the job done, but there have been changes in production and you have to use some tricky workarounds in certain areas. You hear a presentation for a new system produced by XYZ and are impressed with the new features and the product overall, but you tell the sale person no, you don't want to buy. This is where a good sale person will try to overcome your objections to figure out how he can make the sale. He knows it's a good product and will help you make money, so he goes to work.

He might start with the price, is it too high? No, you already know that the upgrade will pay for itself. Is it your old system, are you locked into a contract? Again, no. Is it the thought of the installation process? And with that question, the salesperson has hit the problem. The last install was a nightmare and your staff had problems learning, and the software had bugs that weren't worked out ... and on and on. Now the salesperson knows how to progress to close this sale.

Let's practice. Get a pad and pen and try one or two of these exercises below. You don't have to do them all at one time. Pick the issues that speak to you and see what happens with the exercise.

The Worry Loop

Overcoming objections is one technique that can be applied to breaking Worry Loops. When you find yourself unable to think about anything but the one problem and how it might or might not play out, pick up your notebook and write. Write down the worry. Next, to that write down why you are worried. That should be followed by what action you can take to alleviate the worry. Then work in your possibilities and scenarios that run through your head and write out possible outcomes.

| The Worry | Why | Action | Outcome |
|---|---|---|---|
| Worried about BFF Tina. | She is in another bad relationship. | Talk to her. | She thinks it will all work out. |
| Still worried about Tina. | This guy monopolizes all of her time. | Offer to pick her up or meet after work. | No, he doesn't want to go out. |
| Getting frustrated with Tina. | She is not making time for me. | Ask her to lunch, or a girl's night | No. Maybe next week. |

|  |  | at the movie. |  |
|---|---|---|---|
| Getting angry with Tina. | STOP |  |  |

Look at your answers to the **Why** question, they aren't really about your BFF in the end, are they? Tina isn't making any time for your friendship which is hurting your feelings and making you angry.

What can you do about that? Nothing. You can only control your thoughts and feelings. It is time for you to find something new and interesting to fill the time you spent with Tina. You don't want to cut her off, she'll probably need you when her relationship with Mr. X fails, but let her go, emotionally. Also, break the cycle of dependence on this one friend.

Over Analyzing

Sounds like it goes hand in hand with overthinking, doesn't it? So, let's put a stop to over-analyzing before it starts. Don't try to solve your problem with Tina; you can't, because you don't control Tina. It might be a case of co-dependency and she has switch partners from you to Mr. X. It also might be that Tina enjoys manipulating others and having gotten bored with you, has moved on. Or it could be a number of other things.

Note what was good about that friendship. Know that you will find other friends with those same attributes and talents but without the emotional baggage. Remember that knowing what the problem really is half the battle. We will look at methods to help you move on in future chapters.

The Mean-Mouth Loop

No one in the world is as good at putting you down, taking you out of trying something new or letting you know you are going to fail as you are. Why is that negative voice running and how do you stop it? Better still, how do you turn it into something positive?

Let's see if we can figure out where this negative talk springs. We will start by taking a look at the past. Usually, there is someone in the past that took a swing at your self-esteem and made a direct hit. This is sometimes referred to as a self-esteem monster.

When a friend of mine first did a similar exercise she discovered a long, lost memory in which her first-grade homeroom teacher was one of her self-esteem monsters. She loved art class and the art teacher always had the students sign their work. In this instance, she signed her name in cursive, something they were not scheduled to learn until second or third grade.

Turns out her older brother was learning how to write in cursive and gave her a lesson, using her name. It was a boost to her self-esteem to learn something her peers had not yet learned.

When handing out the artwork at the end of the week, the homeroom teacher would hold up each piece for the class to admire before handing it back. This week, she called my friend up to the head of the class, holding the artwork. My friend was so excited that she was getting special recognition. The teacher asked the other students to note that this student had signed her name in cursive, a subject not yet covered. Then the teacher tore the picture in two and handed the pieces to my friend. She was devastated. Her precious work of art was ruined by a teacher! She was deliberately humiliated in front of all her friends.

In time she forgot the event. But over the years she couldn't understand why she dreaded being called upon in class (all the way through college and beyond) to answer questions. It all came flooding back when she did an exercise similar to the one below. She was terrified of being set up and cut down in front of everyone.

Shame is a powerful emotion and can warp lives if left alone to spread doubt and fear throughout all of our thoughts.

Take your time with this exercise. You may not want to do it until tomorrow or next week. Catch your Mean-Mouth Loop running and listen carefully.

When you are ready, with your pad and pen draw the following grid and fill in the negative talk that always seems to derail your thought process.

| The Mean Talk | Who was this? | Action | Outcome |
|---|---|---|---|
| You know you'll never finish that project? (Let's say you are | What project didn't get finished? Who nagged | Pretend you are writing a letter to this person. | Did you start the project or go to the mechanic? It's okay if |

| | | | |
|---|---|---|---|
| thinking about doing your own tune-up on your car) | or teased you about it? | Tell this person how you are going to go about finishing this project. Layout your plan. | you chose the mechanic; it takes time to erase the negative talk. |
| Are you going to feel comfortable in that outfit? (you are trying a different | Who was your negative fashion police? | Again, write a note to this person telling him/her why you | Did you buy the garment and wear it to work, meeting or social get- |

| look) | | love the outfit and how it looks on you. | together? |
|-------|--|------------------------------------------|-----------|

Did you find any self-esteem monsters from the past? Keep these notes as we will refer to them in future chapters.

~ All men are frightened. The more intelligent they are, the more they are frightened ~

- George S. Patton

Eviction Notice!

Do you find yourself second or triple guessing yourself? Rechecking your math or reasoning to a solution? Compulsively checking again and again? Or perhaps dissecting and exploring a conversation or incident over and over? You can't distract yourself so spend twenty minutes or so figuring out what's going on.

Let's take a moment to look at mean-mouth loop what we referred to up above as the self-esteem monster. These are negative voices from your past that have found a home in your head. Guess what? It's time to evict these monsters. For the most part, you are going to find that what you thought was a bone-crushing T-Rex is really a little chameleon.

Don't just push the mute button on these critical voices. Silence them forever! We will build on the exercise above and learn how to stop these voices later in the book. For now, keep noting these critical voices in your notes. Whenever an "I can't" pops into your thoughts, if it is critical of your abilities, write it down and know that you will deal with it later.

Talk to Your Physician

It is important to keep your physician up-to-date on any changes you are making with diet and exercise. It's also a good idea to keep them in the loop if you are having any symptoms of anxiety.

Your physician might be able to suggest some medication that will help quiet your mind and enhance the self-help exercises you are doing in these chapters. They are also the main reference source for finding a counselor if you need a recommendation. Let them know about any mood swings you might have. Doesn't matter if they are black moods that last for weeks or the occasional blues, tell your physician about them and together you can figure out what is going on to cause these mood swings.

Do Not Suffer in Silence

One of the biggest fallacies surrounding any type of emotional issue is the feeling that you alone are suffering these feelings. You most certainly are not alone! When a friend opened up about some childhood abuse, she had suffered, she was astounded to find that about one in every three women she shared with had a similar experience.

If you feel there is no possible way your dark thoughts and feeling can ever disappear, know that they can. These feelings are shared by many and can come about for a variety of reasons - environmental, biological, genetic, and more. Don't feel that because you can't solve the puzzle of why you have all this static in your brain that you are a failure or weak. You are strong and with the right education and help you can learn how to take control of your thoughts and emotions.

It is very tempting to ignore what you are feeling and carry on as if nothing is wrong like we do with a cold. It comes, you feel bad, it goes only in this case we are talking about your mind you might just be afraid you'll lose it! That is a natural reaction to wanting to stay in control. Interestingly, when you start to let go and let someone help you is the point when you start to gain control.

When you become more accepting of your situation and feel comfortable sharing with others, I hope you will. Being an advocate and spreading awareness of anxiety and depression will help others out of the box in which you were once trapped.

Find your voice. Dealing with your overthinking and stress will help you find your voice. Below are a few signs that you may not be using your voice.

Dissatisfaction with your life. You don't feel like you are living it on your terms.

Others take credit for your work or ideas.

Often you get stuck with the work others don't want

You find yourself doing what others in the group want and not what you had planned.

The background survey you completed and the core values exercise in chapter 3 are will be valuable information for finding your voice.

Practice being assertive. Not aggressive, but assertive. Start small with text to friends to meet for lunch or a coffee. Or reach out to a trusted friend when you are feeling blue and tell them you need some company. A text such as: "I've been in a blue place today and need to break out of it. You have time for dinner and a walk?" Speak to others directly. Look them in the eye, show emotion on your face. Speak calmly but clear, not loud or whiney. Stand up for your needs. If you are interrupted and shut out of a conversation try saying "I would appreciate it if you would let me finish what I was saying before telling us your story."

If you are finding yourself in the dumps regularly, make an appointment to see your physician. Be honest with your physician, he can't help if he doesn't know what's really happening. If you think you are having issues with self-medicating and need help with smoking, drinking, or medication cessation let your physician know. If you are too embarrassed to tell your family physician, find an organization such as Alcoholics Anonymous and get started kicking the habit.

~ Since our society equates happiness with youth, we often assume that sorrow, quiet desperation, and hopelessness go hand in hand with getting older. They don't. Emotional pain or numbness is symptoms of living the wrong life, not a long life. ~

- Martha Beck ~

What Triggers Your Overthinking

Most of us are familiar with memory triggers that use our five senses to help us recall memories. The sight of a red radio flyer wagon; the smell of freshly baked bread, new-mown grass; hearing a certain piece of music, or the touch of a Chenille bedspread might be triggers for many people.

Typically, that is not the kind of trigger that is going to cause overthinking or anxiety. We might see a funeral procession and miss our own loved one for a minute, but that view of a hearse alone is not usually enough to cause an emotional trigger.

Hidden Memories

An emotional trigger is an event that causes a person to remember something traumatic that happened to that person in the past. You might be cruising through your day getting concentrating on the tasks at hand and you overhear a co-worker criticizing another co-worker. Now, your co-workers are not gossiping about you, but it triggers negative emotions and throws you off your game for the rest of the day.

Emotional triggers can be as individual as fingerprints, or they can be shared because of a traumatic event experienced by many. Some typical triggers are public speaking or performing. Receiving an invitation to a shower, wedding, or family reunion. Maybe the thought of asking for a raise cranks up your Mean-Mouth Loop.

This is a partial list of actions that might act as emotions triggers for you:

Someone trying to control you

Rejection

Being the recipient of blame or shame

A smothering or needy person

A friend too busy to make time for you

Judgmental or critical comments

An unexpected sexual advance

Being left (or someone threatening to leave)

Being discounted or ignored

Feeling helpless in a painful situation

Someone appearing unhappy or aloof when you greet them

Do you have recurring dreams about something from your past? Are you uncomfortable in certain rooms? Is there a smell that sets you on edge? These are all examples of emotional triggers.

Do not shy away from these emotional triggers. The sooner you identify and deal with them the sooner you will feel free to move on. It is better to learn to live with the pain of these memories than to bury them deep where they fester.

As you work on your triggers make a note if you find yourself going for any avoidance techniques such as:

You blame others for your pain

You fall back on bad habits or addiction - food, smoking, alcohol, drugs, sex, porn, spending money, work, or gambling to name a few.

You find yourself getting angry or needy

You shut down and are unable to have fun or be around others

You ignore the trigger warning and comply - a people pleaser

If at any time during these exercises you suspect some old trauma that may be holding you back from living a full life make an appointment with your physician and talk to him about a referral for counseling. These can be very difficult memories to confront on your own.

~ The wounded recognized the wounded. ~

- Nora Roberts, Rising Tides
Sliding Doors

The following is an example of a case involving an old trauma long forgotten resurfaced during a home renovation. The old family homestead needed to be sold and the sister responsible for family matters decided to rehab the house prior to putting it on the market.

During the remodeling, the sister was determined to get rid of this one pocket door in the children's bath. The contractor advised against trying a different type of door due to the configuration of the hallway and adjoining rooms. The contractor finally won out and the pocket door stayed with an upgraded look.

The stress of clearing out and selling the family house had led the sibling to get some help from a counselor. In one meeting, she happened to mention the door episode to her counselor in passing, she thought. But the counselor picked up that the sliding door was a trigger for a much larger issue. Turns out a family member had tried repeatedly to get into the bathroom when the sister was showering or on the toilet. She would have to push desperately against the door (there was no lock) to keep this person from entering. Sometimes sopping wet, still in the shower, leaning out to keep the door pulled shut. She had buried these attempted assaults for years. All these years she had a dislike of sliding doors of any kind and didn't understand why.

This is why I will keep encouraging you to think about counseling during the exercises. Sometimes we deliberately don't remember trauma so that we can get on with our lives. Oppressing difficult memories is a coping mechanism in its own right. It works very well for a while. Protecting us from memories that might otherwise lead to major depression or suicide. But, at some point, the trauma must be dealt with or we will suffer even more from the stress produced.

Positive and Negative

Below is an example of the Emotional Trigger exercise. The idea is to get a list of items that evoke certain emotions. We will use this list in later exercises.

| Emotional Triggers | | |
| --- | --- | --- |
| | | |
| **Interest** | | **Joy** |
| Music, dance | | The perfect taste |
| Learning a new skill | | Playing chase |
| | | Jumping in a pile of leaves |
| | | |
| **Fear** | | **Sadness** |
| Blind dates | | Wasted time |
| Barking dogs | | A misunderstanding from the past |
| Bad dreams | | |
| | | |
| | | |
| **Love** | | **Comfort** |

| Old friends | | Salt breeze |
|---|---|---|
| Stroll through a garden | | Scent of gladiolas |
| | | |
| | | |
| **Anger** | | **Guilt** |
| Laziness | | Betraying a trust |
| Gross negligence | | Gossip |
| | | |

On a new page from your notebook copy the above chart. There is also a blank form in Chapter 8 labeled Emotional Triggers. Write down the first word or phrase you think of that brings out each emotion. If you are having a hard time starting, there is a list of possible trigger words in Chapter 8 below the chart.

## Chapter 4: Overcoming Panic And Anxiety

There are numerous techniques utilized by individuals which have effectively helped them conquered panic and anxiety in their own lives. Huge numbers of these strategies are inside your very own control and are useful to you; they'll easily be incorporated into your life in all respects effectively.

These methods of coping with panic and anxiety help plan to adjust your psyche and your observations about 'reality'. A portion of these procedures includes retraining the brain and body to act and carry on in an alternate manner when you are stood up with the idea of panicking or feeling anxiety.

The main strategy that can enable you to conquer panic and anxiety in your life is ordinary exercise. Numerous individuals are unconscious of the incredible mental advantages that can be gained from normal exercise. Exercise is incredible for passionate recharging. As a rule the manner in which we are thinking can straightforwardly corresponded with the manner in which we are feeling.

On the off chance that we have low vitality and are feeling lazy, at that point this will influence your psychological prosperity. Your degrees of eagerness might be decreased and you may feel like you have an absence of center and drive.

In some cases, negative contemplatives can emerge out of inclination, substantial, and torpid within. Exercise is likewise extraordinary for discharging any strain that has been developed within. It is additionally known for discharging glad synthetic concoctions inside the mind.

Another extraordinary device you can use to help beat anxiety and panic is rehearsing unwinding procedures. Unwinding strategies help stop your mind from dashing with negative considerations and works to calm the brain. At times all you have to do is not focus on the ongoing contemplation that your brain is bringing to the surface and rather focus on the positive sentiments going on in your body.

There are numerous unwinding sounds that are valuable at helping you arrive at significant degrees of relax, both in the body and the psyche. A few sounds utilize guided symbolism to loosen up you and different sounds utilize controlled and centered breathing to help focus and adjust you to the intrinsic prosperity that is in every case promptly accessible to you when you experience it.

At the point when the body and brain are encountering prosperity, the considerations in your mind will in general become progressively positive and stick to this same pattern with positive sentiments.

Another extraordinary strategy that enables individuals to beat panic and anxiety is spellbinding. It involves controlling the customer into an adjusted condition of mindfulness, where the hypnotherapist can help encourage change in where they access their internal mental assets that can be used to defeat their issues.

A REAL CURE FOR PANIC ATTACKS AND ANXIETY

Everyone has encountered anxiety at one time or another; it is our normal human reaction to fear. In any case, if panic and stress have assumed responsibility for your life, you might experience the ill effects of an anxiety issue.

Numerous individuals seek prescriptions as an answer to extreme anxiety or panic assaults. While drugs can calm numerous anxiety side effects, they don't fix the hidden issue and it's commonly not a decent long haul arrangement. The uplifting news is, there are approaches to defeat panic and anxiety without drugs. Numerous anxiety medicines are accessible to enable you to lessen anxiety's side effects and recapture control of your life.

Understanding anxiety drugs

There is a wide range of drugs used to treat anxiety issues. They incorporate sedatives (Xanax, Ativan, Valium), antidepressants (Zoloft, Paxil, Lexapro), and beta-blockers (Inderal and Atenolol). Any of these prescriptions can be powerful in alleviating the indications of panic and anxiety, however they shouldn't be considered as a remedy for the genuine issue.

Physician endorsed medications can give brief alleviation, yet they can't treat the hidden reasons for anxiety issues. Without tending to the hidden reasons, your anxiety indications can return in full power once you've quit taking the prescription.

Dangers of anxiety meds

Anxiety meds can accompany various horrendous and even hazardous symptoms. Many can be addictive, making it hard to quit taking them once you've begun. Others can take half a month to create the ideal help. It is essential to recollect that while anxiety prescriptions can be useful, they're not by any means the only answer.

Elective treatment decisions for anxiety

There are numerous treatment options in contrast to doctor-prescribed medications. One amazing model is intellectual social treatment, which is, for the most part, is accepted to be the best treatment for anxiety and panic issues. CBT centers around distinguishing and revising negative idea designs which cause us to stress and panic, and show more advantageous, increasingly positive approaches to adapt to life's worries.

To conquer anxiety forever, real changes in your way of life are fundamental. Way of life changes that reduce anxiety incorporates standard exercise, sufficient rest, and keeping up a solid eating regimen.

At any rate, 30 minutes of oxygen consuming activity consistently can diminish physical and passionate pressure;

47

being all around rested empowers us to adapt better to everyday obligations and stresses; while eating a solid eating regimen that joins products of the soil and takes out caffeine and refined sugar can re-establish the cerebrum's serotonin levels and in this manner decline anxiety.

Preferences of elective treatments

The main bit of leeway with non-sedate anxiety medicines is that they make enduring positive changes and long haul alleviation. In the event that you end up battling with panic and anxiety, in spite of using anxiety drugs, there is an approach to end this horrible cycle and defeat anxiety without the utilization of prescriptions and there is a program accessible to show you how.

TECHNIQUES TO BEAT PANIC AND ANXIETY ATTACKS

Anxiety has turned out to be one of the world's most basic psychological sicknesses. Some people only experience gentle assaults while others experience the complete ill effects of serious anxiety. The individuals who endure the latter are bound to have panic and anxiety assaults that reason some hindering side effects include, peevishness, extreme perspiring, eagerness, sickness, cerebral pains, trembling, rest aggravations, weakness, rest unsettling influences, and significantly more. It has been discovered that such circumstances possibly deteriorate if the individual isn't equipped for controlling their musings.

In any case, there have additionally been ways also observed to be powerful in adapting to and conquering panic induced anxiety assaults. Strategies and procedures have been explored and created to counter anxiety assaults and keep them from deteriorating. One basic of a method for battling such assaults is to occupy yourself. This is, in any case, compelling just if the assault is as yet mellow and is simply starting to deteriorate. It's done essentially by calling somebody, perusing some mitigating verse, conversing with somebody or by tuning in to loosening up music which will successfully enable you to divert your negative considerations while simultaneously giving a quiet and alleviating impact.

In certain motion pictures we regularly find in certain motion pictures, another method for defeating panic or anxiety assaults is by continuing quiet explanations to yourself or some mantra. This may make you look idiotic at the same time, but the procedure is equally as successful as the first referenced. Helping yourself to remember having been in a similar circumstance and that nothing terrible happened will enable you to quiet yourself; accordingly, keeping the assault from deteriorating.

Should that you observe such method to be somewhat hard to do now and again when it is required the most, one flawless option is to just record all the positive musings and assertions on list cards or on little bits of paper which you can keep with you in your wallet, pack, satchel, or bag. Whenever you get the chance to feel an anxiety assault developing, you can just effectively take out the notes and read the announcements to quiet your musings.

Anxiety, as we know, is in some cases only a result of negative contemplations. On the off chance that one is fit for controlling their brain, at that point anxiety assaults can be effectively anticipated. It is each of the matter of molding one's brain or changing one's perspective. Having the option to ace your considerations we also bring you above and beyond in adapting to your anxiety assaults as well as to defeat the anxiety itself viably. Time is additionally an essential segment in helping you beat your anxiety assaults. Essentially setting aside an effort to learn and ace these self-improvement techniques for anxiety assaults will enable you to recapture control of your life making your initial step to a voyage towards full recuperation.

HELP FOR PANIC ATTACK AND ANXIETY

For individuals who are inclined to anxiety, panic assaults can strike whenever. Whenever left untreated, it might form into an incessant issue that later on may be increasingly hard to fix and oversee. It is smarter to get help for panic assault and anxiety issues at the beginning instead of evading the thought till later and imagining that it will blur away without anyone else.

Help for panic assault and anxiety at the early stages is additionally much easier and less touchy than that of the more created cases. As anticipation is additionally superior to anything fixed, there are circumstances and things that can be maintained a strategic distance from to avoid panic assault scenes.

The principal thing one needs to do is get help from a companion or close relative or an individual whom you think really cares about you. Including other individuals in your circumstance, it reduces your emotional weight and helps you appropriately conquer the condition. To request the individual's help, you'll have to let them know or her the entire story; be honest and legit about the issue. Avoid being baffled in case that the person thinks that it's less genuinely than the individual in question should. Give the individual time to thoroughly consider it and for the person in question to understand that the issue is something that you both need to take into genuine thought.

Next, to get help for panic assaults and anxiety, you'll have to recognize the main driver of your concerns. Comprehend what you dread and consider the explanation for that dread. You additionally need to share those contemplations with your companion. Ask their interpretation of it. As a general rule, the individual will reveal to you that you don't need to fear that and will likely disclose to you a few reasons why. Try not to accept it as contrarily. Keep in mind that the individual you requested help from is truly attempting to assist you with your concerns. Rather, tune in to what the person in question is stating. Truth be told, the greater part of what individuals state about your dread is valid and bringing them into the center will enable you to be increasingly reasonable about the circumstance or about what you dread. For instance, say you have an extraordinary dread of heights. You likely experienced tumbling from an earlier time or saw somebody falling and the trauma prompts something terrible. Presumably, your companion will disclose to you that it is generally typical to fear statures, yet it's not worth panic over it and to give that dread a chance to prevent you from doing things like intersecting an extension or climbing the stairs. Know and understand that you can assume responsibility for the circumstance by taking additional consideration or by having somebody go with you as a helpful guide throughout.

In conclusion, help for panic assault and anxiety can be found by looking for restorative consideration after a couple of intermittent scenes. An expert will probably enable you to beat the condition quicker and all the more successfully.

How Pregnant Women Can Cope

Being pregnant is quite often a very on edge time in a lady's life. This bodes well since there are numerous sound apprehensions and worries that are straightforwardly connected with both birth and pregnancy. Hence, pregnant ladies will in general experience the ill effects of a particularly high number of panic assaults and anxiety issues.

Regardless of whether anxiety and panic assaults are related to issues before pregnancy, after pregnancy, or baby blues, women would be astute to illuminate themselves about how to adapt to panic assaults. Ladies are frequently totally overpowered with pressure during pregnancy; the circumstance is awful for the individuals who are regularly worriers.

Adjusting Joy, Positivity, and Negativity

Keep in mind that pressure does not come only from negative sources; positive occasions also triggers worry also. Since the pregnancy produces huge measures of happiness just as tremendous apprehensions, it achieves a lot of pressure.

Luckily, adapting to the anxiety and panic assaults identified with pregnancy does not need to be troublesome. A pregnant lady needs to pursue some simple advances that will help her in de-focusing and conquering any potential panic assaults. She ought to likewise do everything she can to teach herself about what she will experience during her nine months of pregnancy.

At the point when a lady finds out about how gainful moderate and profound breathing is, she will be progressively arranged to deal with anxiety. When she gets restless, she should simply to gradually take a full breath while she puts her left hand on her stomach. This straightforward action quiets the psyche and causes it to focus on an option that is other than pressure.

What a lady eats and drinks can likewise influence her feelings of anxiety. An eating regimen that is loaded with organic products, vegetables, and proteins is certain to help with adapting to panic assaults. Proteins should originate from lean meats, fish, poultry, and egg whites. This sort of eating regimen likewise advances a sentiment of smoothness.

Getting a decent night's rest is additionally an incredible path for a pregnant lady to manage her elevated feelings of pressure and anxiety. A total night of value rest encourages a lady to understand the pressure that she has encountered for the duration of the day. Resting soundly has endless preferable pressure diminishing abilities over any medicine that a lady could take.

## Chapter 5: What Are Positive Affirmations

### And How Can We Use Them?

Consider your childhood. Were you surrounded by love and affection? Did you have a happy childhood and form lasting bonds with friends at school? If you had an idyllic childhood, then why do you have negative feelings about yourself and fail to realize your own potential?

The answer lies in our cultural heritage. The feelings of fear and guilt if you didn't conform come from guardians and authority and unless you had amazing people telling you how special you were then these feelings will follow you into adulthood.

It is rare for a child to be encouraged to be unique and special. Instead, we are taught to follow the rules and be obedient, you may dare to dream but society teaches you that these dreams will remain unfulfilled.

So, how can you become a fiercely positive being who lives life to the full and casts aside negative thoughts? Using affirmations may seem a little off the wall but telling yourself to be positive can be an uplifting process and ultimately increase your happiness and confidence in less than a week.

Affirmations should be used in the present tense and if possible, should be said loudly and consciously. Embrace the words that you use and believe in them!

Here are some situations that may arise and some suitable affirmations to use

When you are feeling insignificant or overwhelmed by life

1)I am a unique citizen of the world

2)I matter and my presence is a gift

3)I have a brightness that shines and casts light on the world

When you are nervous

1)I am strong enough to get through this

2)I am able to breathe in calmness and exhale nervousness

3)I believe in myself and my ability to shine

When you are angry

1)I can visualize my anger and let it go

2)I am able to replace my anger with positive emotions

3)I accept responsibility for my anger, but I can forgive myself

When you feel hopeless and at the end of your tether

1)I accept the situation and will try to find a positive aspect

2)I possess the optimism to find hope in any situation

3)I will explore all ways of coping

4)If I have exhausted my options I will ask for help, this is not a weakness

5)I have inner courage that helps me cope

When you are with people you love

1)I am surrounded by people who love me and respect me

2)I feel safe and respected among my friends

3)I take the time to show my friends what they mean to me

4)I enjoy the differences in opinions we all have and respect their beliefs

5)I don't judge others and my friends do not judge me

When you are among strangers

1)I am smart and good company; these people are in for a treat

2)I am sure I am going to meet someone amazing today

3)If I feel the need to leave, I have the confidence to do so

4)I see myself as a gift to the world

5)I refuse to compare myself to anyone for I don't know their whole story

When you can't face the day ahead

1)I choose to give this day my full consideration and face it with joy

2)My mind is capable of creating a bright new day

3)This day holds no fears and will bring me nothing but happiness

When people are unsupportive to your dreams

1)I will answer questions about my dreams without becoming defensive

2)I accept the choices of others but will not let them affect me pursuing my dreams

3)I follow dreams no matter what the obstacles

When you are at work

1)I choose to work here, and I find the work fulfilling and enjoyable

2)I am responsible for my career success and see myself advancing through my own hard work

3)My job impacts other people in a good way

4)I can influence others with my experience

5)I am a key part of a successful operation

When you can't sleep

1)I thank my mind for all its great work during the day

2)I now release my mind from thinking and wish it a good night

3)I am surrounded by the peace and quiet of the night

4)I look forward to the pleasant dreams that await me

5)A full night's peaceful sleep lays ahead

When you are sad and lonely

1)I am surrounded by the love of those who are not physically present

2)Solitude is a gift and allows me to enjoy my own company

3)I am too big a gift to the world to feel sadness or self-pity

When you are tempted to give up

1)Giving up is an easy option and I am better than the easy option

2)I will carry on because I believe in the task, I am attempting

3)My goals have no time limit and it is too early to contemplate giving up

4)I know what lies ahead is worth the effort so I will press on

5)I am willing to try every conceivable option

When you doubt yourself

1)I am not just good enough; I am better than that

2)I approve of myself and that is all that matters

3)I no longer have the habit of self-criticism

4)I am able to see the benefits of my flaws and my personal gifts

5)I have a positive mindset and am able to praise myself

When you feel stuck in a rut

1)I know the answer is available to me, I just need to keep looking

2)I am actively looking for ways to change my situation

3)My abilities will help me unlock the way and set me on a new path

4)I have the courage to try a path that is completely new

5)My mind will always embrace new ideas and concepts

When you recognize your own awesomeness

1)I leave behind my past; it has no power over me now

2)Everything I need will become available to me at the right time and place in my existence

3)My heart and my mind have a rhythm that flows, and I embrace it fully

4)I am gifted and talented, I matter to myself and others

5)I am deeply fulfilled with my life and who I am

These phrases will help you leave behind the negative feelings that can hold you back. You can also use them to inspire you in the home or workplace. Most furniture or décor stores will have bright colorful signs that you can hang on your walls, here are a few personal favorites that hang in my home:

• Follow your heart
• Create peace
• Dream big

- Enjoy the little things
- Hug often
- Do your best
- Say I love you
- Laugh at yourself
- Be spontaneous
- Fall in love
- Show gratitude

## Chapter 6: Over Thinking Affliction That

## Affects Many

Many of us are affected by a terrible affliction, a disease that causes suffering and misery in billions of people. The most amazing symptom of this disease is that most people don't even know that they have it. Other symptoms include headaches, stress, restlessness, heartburn, ulcers, and other digestive issues, loss of sleep, shortness of breath, memory loss, low self-esteem, substance abuse, and absent-mindedness. It is a condition loosely described as "obsessive thinking." This is not to be confused with obsessive compulsive disorder, although I believe the two are linked.

As I trudge the path of happy destiny, I oftentimes notice my mind churning endlessly about minutiae, known as "pole vaulting over mouse turns." Endlessly asking "what if, "my mind reviews and replays every event in my life to squeeze every possible nuance and possibility out of each memory, no matter how insignificant or overwhelming it might be. I analyze everything into an exhaustive state, as if chewing on each memory will change it or make me happier. As I engage in this totally useless activity, I beat myself up second guessing my past actions or thought processes.

As if constantly dissecting my memories were not enough, I also fantasize about how various scenarios will play out depending on what I say or do. I obsessively fantasize about how things can go wrong and what I can do to prevent it. This is taking worrying to a whole new level. I also describe it as "worst case scenario thinking"

Thousands of years ago our ancestors 'biggest concerns were which end of the food chain they found themselves. It made an life or death difference whether people could perceive and analyze warning signs such as dinosaur poop or raptor tracks. Being ready to instantly react to signs of danger were defense mechanisms that helped prolong life. The problem is that the dangers of being eaten no longer exist, but the defense mechanism continues to run and has evolved into obsessive analysis of what is being perceived around us.

When we engage in " worst case scenario" thinking, we perceive everything as a potential threat and continually analyze this data in order to hopefully overcome these perceived threats. We project an infinite number of possibilities and permutations into the distant future, worrying about how life will turn out or avoiding possible pitfalls. Our brains act like computers who are continuously running on an "loop" with no possible conclusion to the program that is running. When we over analyze and think too much, we cut ourselves off from the two of our most powerful survival tools, instinct and intuition.

To make matters worse, when we engage in these thinking patterns, oftentimes we get so wrapped up with what is happening in our minds that we forget to breathe. Some people stop breathing for long periods of time as their analytical brains take over. When this happens, oxygen ceases to flow to our frontal lobes and we fall into crisis mode known as " monkey brain." At that point we only have two choices, to run away or fight.Neither choice is needed in today's world, although it was quite handy when we found ourselves to face with a saber-toothed tiger.

Analytical thinking is useful when planning a war or programming a computer. It sucks when it comes to dealing with relationships and our personal issues. The more we think about our past, and analyzing our actions, etc., the more we suffer. The more we engage in "worst case scenario"

Thinking the more we suffer. The more that we wish things were different, the more we suffer

The more we compare ourselves to others, the more we suffer. The more we second-guess ourselves, the more we suffer. The more we beat ourselves up, the more we suffer.

The more we suffer, the more stress we create in our lives that in turn creates the medical problems listed above. We are literally " thinking ourselves to death." So what do we do? How do we think less and feel more? There are some very simple exercises to heal this disease. First detach from your thoughts. The mantra is "I am not my thoughts." A good meditation is to sit in front of an empty chair, and imagine yourself in that chair looking back at you. The more you can visualize yourself sitting in that empty chair looking at you, the easier it will be to detach to your thinking

Second, get some exercise. It is impossible to engage in analytical thinking while you are gasping fro breath. The endorphins that are releases in your brain as a result of exercise are powerful chemicals that create a euphoric feeling and slow down obsessive thinking. Third, eat

Healthy foods. When your body is happy, you do not need to engage in survival thinking and your mind will slow down. I notice that eating unprocessed food (raw) makes me feel much better about myself and slows down my thinking. When I am on the road eating truck stop food, my mind goes berserk. Fourth, focus on your breathing. Breathe long and slow breaths at all times. Yogi masters tell us that we are given an finite number of breaths in our lives. When we breathe long and slow breaths, we live longer happier lives. Fifth, drink more water. Dehydration causes the mind to go into crisis mode. Sixth, practice gratitude and forgiveness of yourself. You

Do not have to forgive anyone else, only yourself. Be grateful for your life and the people in it.

## Chapter 7: Understanding And Managing, Processing, And Embracing Negative Emotions

As positive psychology has expanded our understanding of our negative emotions, it's similarly been able to outfit us with various strategies for modifying these emotions in our daily lives.

Sims (2017) examined ways to deal with negative emotions proactively by acknowledging negative emotions; he devised the contraction TEARS of HOPE to help coach and guide individuals, which is described below in greater detail.

T = Teach and Learn

This is the path toward checking out what your body is trying to tell you through the presentation of negative emotions; it is better to acknowledge what these emotions mean. This builds your one-of-a-kind understanding of the way you respond to emotional states by allowing you to decipher the sign your body is sending you and determine what purpose this emotion fills.

E = Express and Enable

Negative emotions urge us to express them. They are actionable emotions. This segment of the acronym urges you to explore your emotions with straightforwardness and curiosity. It's connected to increasing the acceptance of your instincts and enabling them to be accessible without scorn.

A= Accept and Become More Acquainted With

This element of the acronym allows you to become more acquainted with yourself and how you are as a human. Focus on increasing your acceptance through positive affirmations to bring your hover of negative emotions into a space of affirmation.

R = Re-Evaluate and Re-Layout

When you accept your emotions as part of your character, you can begin to focus on reframing the condition and how you react. Just because an antagonistic inclination has risen doesn't mean that you have to react in a way that will have negative effects on you and individuals around you.

Enduring antagonistic emotions isn't a way of maintaining, tolerating, or making excuses for poor habits or practices; it's a way of caring for oneself and improving our reactions to other individuals

S = Social Assistance

Understanding that negative emotions are accessible in every single one of us, and, for all intents and purposes, in a comparative way, can be a magnificent wellspring of compassion and sympathy to everybody around us. It's how we process our emotions that makes the difference, so watching someone in the throes of shock and understanding that they are essentially dealing with an obvious peril can encourage us to approach them with compassion, rather than shock ourselves.

H = Hedonic Success and Happiness

This is the route toward replacing our negative social experiences with positive ones. Since we, as a whole, are more likely to survey negative experiences immediately, it might be helpful for us to bundle them with positive experiences so that we don't fall into a ruminating trap. Consequently, we can focus more on assessing positive experiences.

O = Observe and Visit

Resist the urge to watch your reactions without ignoring them, suppressing them, or overly distorting them. Use care to convey your focus to your mind and body and what particular inclination that it is producing inside you. Deal with these reactions without judgment.

P = Physiology and Social Changes

As you watch your enthusiastic and mental responses, watch your physiological reactions, too. Focus on your breath, your heartbeat, and try to figure out the modifications in your physiology that a negative inclination may have caused. Resist the urge to judge these modifications in your physiology.

E = Eudaimonia

This presumably won't be a word you think about; anyway, it's well worth adding to your language. Eudaimonia is a Greek word that essentially implies having a better-than-average soul. It occurs when you have found a state of being that is merry, strong and prosperous, and you have made sense of how to partake in exercises that result in your general thriving. It means that you're successfully trying to feel that all that you do is meaningful and valid.

I've encountered the assessments available and, moreover, assembled the underlying tips to empower you to supervise and provide you with the methods to handle negative emotions and develop habits that will help you to understand them and motivate yourself to improve your emotional state.

EXERCISES

Practicing gratitude has been deemed to have marvellous effects for both the recipients and providers. These effects have along-lasting impact on our perspective on events and life in general.

Whether it's an easily-overlooked detail or a significant thing, telling someone face to face or by phone, a letter, or a text how much that you appreciate something that they have done, can genuinely impact the way that you see and respond to negative emotions.

Use the TEARS of HOPE course to understand why you may respond to events, individuals, or situations the way that you do. Self-care can empower you to find the headspace to do this positively.

Understand How to Respond, Rather Than React

Do you know the difference between how you respond versus how you react?

Negative emotions, much of the time, encourage us to react quickly to a given circumstance. When we feel irate, we may lash out or holler. These negative reactions may have many drawbacks; we may, for example, repel the people around us.

By exploring your negative emotions, you can start to develop an awareness of when you are reacting negatively and adapt more positive strategies for responding — in some cases, this could mean realizing that no reaction (in any way, shape, or form) is required.

Acknowledge When to Take a Break.

Acknowledge when to take a day to yourself. If you are continually experiencing negative emotions and endeavouring to direct them, your body is revealing to you that something isn't right. Take a day to re-center. Fill this day with positive experiences, achieving the things that you know fuel you and make you feel better. This kind of break can help you to realign your thinking, give you some space to refocus on why you may experience negative emotions, and devise some positive strategies for adjusting your behavior.

This is just a quick summary of the tips that I feel would be most valuable; some tips may work better for you than others. Everything comes down to you as an individual. Some of these tips may work genuinely well and others, not so much. Assess two or three different methods and find the ones that work best for you.

## Chapter 8: Effects Of A Cluttered Mind

## Over Time

There are different ways in which clutter affects you over time. This is because it has an impact on various aspects of your life that affects how you live an approach different challenges that you will have to face.

Clutter Harms Your Health

Your home is not the main thing influenced by over-aggregation of stuff. Clutter additionally has demonstrated, substantial impacts on your psychological and physical prosperity.

1. Clutter triggers respiratory issues.

As indicated by different researchers, cluttered homes regularly contain more residue, which can cause or enhance breathing issues. As more things heap up, more residue is produced. This makes the perfect living condition for vermin like residue parasites. The harder it gets the opportunity to get to various territories of the home to clean, the more genuine these respiratory issues become.

2. Clutter wrecks your eating regimen.

Research in the United States found that members in an efficient domain picked more advantageous snacks than those in a cluttered situation. Clutter is upsetting for the brain, so you are bound to depend on ways of dealing with stress, for example, picking comfort meals or overeating than if you invest energy in a neater environment.

3. Clutter expands your pressure.

As indicated by an investigation concentrating on human science and character, individuals with cluttered homes loaded with incomplete tasks were progressively discouraged, exhausted, and had more elevated amounts of the pressure hormone cortisol than the individuals who depicted their homes as peaceful and remedial. The research additionally makes reference to that cortisol's inability to decay regularly over the course of the day has been related with more prominent interminable pressure, malady movement, and even mortality hazard.

4. Clutter undermines your security.

Restorative experts caution that exorbitant measures of clutter — particularly cardboard boxes, paper, and garments — can square entryways and windows, making a genuine flame peril.

Clutter Hurts Your Relationships

On the off chance that you share your home with others, extreme clutter is never again only a "you" issue. Clutter in your home can likewise contrarily affect the lives of your better half and children.

5. Clutter imperils your adoration life.

Individuals with accumulating issue steadily experience issues disposing of things in view of an apparent need to spare them. They likewise feel upset at the idea of separating with their possessions. This can negatively affect one's marriage, as studies have demonstrated that impulsive hoarders have higher rates of separation.

Clutter's negative effect on marriage is not constrained to hoarders. Companions of a cluttered individual who are disturbed by the state of nature express their uneasiness in judgment, negative remarks, ridiculing, outrage and peevishness.

6. Clutter disturbs your children.

On the off chance that you have children, they also can feel the negative impacts of a cluttered home. The National Institute of Mental Health found that children living in a seriously cluttered condition frequently have raised degrees of trouble, encountering not so much joy but rather more trouble making companions.

7. Clutter disconnects you.

The tidiness of your home can influence your longing to welcome anybody into it. In a scientific review, a large portion of studied property holders said they won't welcome companions over if their house is cluttered.

Do whatever it takes not to go excessively far the other way, however. Living in an overly clean and controlled condition can likewise cause pressure, which damages your musculoskeletal, respiratory, cardiovascular, endocrine, and gastrointestinal framework. As indicated by various logical researches, that degree of uneasiness makes it difficult for somebody to go out in light of the fact that he/she is so engrossed with whether it is slick enough.

Clutter Affects Your Career

On the off chance that an individual does not have power over their home condition, they use the function as a break. Individuals with chaotic inclinations once in a while keep their confusion to simply their homes. This implies bedlam can saturate your professional life, as well.

8. Clutter keeps you from getting advanced.

A confused work area, a chaotic satchel or handbag, and a vague documenting framework or no recording framework at all would all be able to majorly affect your activity execution. An investigation regarding the matter found that 30% of businesses are less inclined to advance somebody with a muddled workspace.

9. Clutter makes you miss work.

Specialists have discovered enthusiastic storing was related to a normal of seven work disability days out of every month — more than those revealed by members with other uneasiness, state of mind, and substance use issue.

10. Clutter diminishes profitability.

At the point when your condition is cluttered, the mayhem hinders your capacity to center. A study by various researchers regarding the matter saw that different boosts present in the visual field simultaneously vie for neural portrayal.

At the end of the day, a work area strewn with papers, snacks, photographs, and pens will likely destroy any sort of efficiency you had made arrangements for the day. The exploration additionally demonstrates that a perfect workplace will enable you to be progressively gainful, less grumpy, and better ready to process data.

Clutter Negatively Impacts Your Finances

An untidy home can adversely influence how you deal with your funds, prompting poor cash the executives and extreme obligation. While there are answers for these issues, having the option to locate your electric bill is a decent spot to begin.

11. Clutter energizes terrible ways of managing money.

At the point when your house is cluttered, it is anything but difficult to lose things. On the off chance that you can't discover a thing, similar to your yoga tangle or your pooch's preferred toy, you may purchase a copy. This propensity joined with spending a great deal of cash to store things, can stray into the red.

12. Clutter keeps you paying off debtors.

A cluttered home can likewise make it hard to find bank proclamations and important bills. Another lost bill prompts another late installment. Abruptly, you are managing extra charges, higher financing costs, or even gathering organizations. Set up programmed bill pay or make schedule reminders in your telephone to guarantee you pay your bills on schedule.

## Chapter 9: You Can Do It!

"Believe in yourself, and the rest will fall into place. Have faith in your own abilities, work hard, and there is nothing you cannot accomplish" **- Brad Henry**

Everything you need to overcome overthinking and its underlying mental conditions such as depression, anxiety, and worry are already inside of you. Live according to your own terms, follow your heart since it already knows the right direction to go accept yourself regardless of your flaws.

How to Follow Your Heart

But in spite of life attempting to pull you in a very million directions, there are ways that you will carve out a sacred house for yourself. You can do your best to measure consistent with your heart's want, which can assist you in getting pleasure from the life you reside and be a lot of gifts to the individuals around you.

Part 1: Identifying Your Heart's Want

Make a list of belongings you wish to accomplish. A "bucket list" can facilitate you fathom that direction your heart desires to travel in. Try to set goals that you just are probably to be ready to accomplish (not "be the primary human on Mars"). This list can be an excellent supply of inspiration once you are checking out significant events to figure toward in your life. If it's truly from the heart, it will replicate a number of your deepest interests and aspirations. Create an associate open house. The first step to going in together with your heart this means is to allow your heart the time and house to talk up. It's important to take a seat still while not distractions for your heart to be ready to let itself be detected. You may wish to form associate intentional place wherever you'll visit simply sit. If you have an additional room in your house, you can lightweight some candles and build a snug atmosphere for this task.

Listen to your heart. Once you've set the right conditions, you can begin to try and do the work of being advertently receptive to your heart. You may wish to raise yourself an issue, such as "what am I feeling under the surface right now?" Wait a short time once you raise the question to examine if a response bubbles up from your heart. This kind of practice can facilitate your heart and your inner desire, express itself.

You can additionally use a method referred to as Focusing, which is nice for obtaining in a bit together with your body. Here's how to do Focusing:

Once you've cleared the house and asked what is going on within you, pay attention to what your body answers with. Don't attempt to explore it; just notice it from a distance. For instance, you may feel a tightness in your chest once you raise what is going on beneath the surface. Notice it from a distance.

Put a handle on the sensation. This is usually within the kind of a word or short phrase. For instance, you can say "tightness" or "chest pressure" or "tension." Keep trying words out till it looks to work the feeling. Go back and forth between the feeling and also the word that describes it. Check and see how they move. See if the body sensation changes a little bit once you have the correct associate name for it.

Ask yourself what is inflicting this sensation. What is it about your life without delay that is inflicting you to feel tight in your chest? do not grasp for a solution, just let the response bubble up. This may not happen the primary time. Focusing can take observe, but this is an excellent series of steps to assist you in opening yourself to your heart and everything that is happening within you.

Set aside time day after day. A hectic life will extremely dampen your ability to follow your heart. Take time out of your day, every day, for yourself. Don't let something else impose on this point. What you do with it's up to you, but here are a few suggestions:

**Meditate.** There is a range of mental and physical health advantages to meditating, such as lower pressure and lower stress. Try sitting upright for at least ten minutes in a very quiet place. Focus on one thing, such as the feeling of air getting into and out of your nostrils, or an object like a pencil. When your attention leaves the object, gently remind yourself to come back. Take a long bath. Relaxing in water has similar effects to alternative relaxation techniques. It's a good way to wind down. You can use this point to replicate on your life, or just get pleasure from the silence and sensation of a heat tub.

Have a coffee date with a friend. You may not get to pay the maximum amount of time catching up with friends as you'd like. Use this "you time" to invite a cherished friend to own lunch or coffee with you.

Find interests that activate your heart. Society places a big stress on the brain. It says that you should "think before you act" and keep rational decisions. However, this doesn't leave a lot of area for your intuition or your heart. These things can build life pleasurable instead of routine and economical. Finding activities that touch your heart will facilitate keep the pathway open, rather than only partaking the planet together with your brain.

For instance, if you like to read, make positive to permit time for reading in your schedule. Ask your friends for recommendations for smartbooks. A poetry collection will be particularly redolent.

If you're a lot of a moving picture buff, check out some highly rated films that may tug on your heartstrings.

Spending time in nature is another smart option; it will facilitate you feel a lot of alive and connected with yourself.

Part 2: Organizing Your Life

Seek medical care if it looks useful. If the problems obstruction you from following your heart appears a lot of serious than you'll upset on your own, or with help from a friend, consider seeing a healer. Many therapists deal with this sort of downside on a daily basis. If you had a traumatic childhood, a bad wedding, or if you've simply folded beneath a ton of stress, therapy will facilitate you discover your heart and feel a lot of alive.

Somatic experiencing medical care is similar to Focusing, where you focus on sensations in your body instead of thoughts and recollections. Cognitive-behavioral therapy will facilitate you examine mounted thoughts and beliefs, which will be preventing you from following your heart.

Ask friends to facilitate. Sometimes it's onerous to break through to wherever your heart is all on your own. Enlist the help of a lover for this task. You can truly do Focusing with a lover, where you go through the steps along and report what happens. You can additionally simply bring up what is going on in your life without delay, and specific you want to urge a lot of connected together with your heart. See if she has any advice for you. Talking it out can additionally facilitate because expressing your emotions in words has a powerful result.

For example, you can say, "Hey, I feel like I'm not extremely following my heart in my life without delay. I could extremely use somebody to speak to regarding this. Would you be willing to help?"

Live your own life. It's easy to measure our lives in response to pressure from others, such as friends, family, a spouse, or even kids. If you want to follow your heart, make positive you're living consistent with your own needs instead of what others wish from you. This is actually one amongst the foremost usually reportable regrets from folks that are on their deathbeds.

Ask yourself, "Is this what I truly wish, or am I doing it for someone else in spite of myself?"

There's nothing wrong with being generous and doing things for alternative individuals, of course, but you have got to seek out a balance wherever you're faithful yourself once you are being kind and serving to others. Otherwise, however, smart your intentions, you can simply give way and lose your affiliation to your heart.

Commit yourself to your path. Changing your mind will be a straightforward answer to adverse things, but if you perpetually back out, you'll ne'er learn from your mistakes or build any progress. It's important to decide on the trail you are on in life. Commitment will offer you the strength to hold on within the face of the issue. Following your heart isn't perpetually presupposed to be simple. If you feel a lot of resistance toward this sort of commitment, whether it's to education or an explicit career, then it might be an honest plan to look at whether or not you are extremely following your heart.

Avoid mistaking natural resistance and issue with this kind of bigger resistance. It's normal to feel pessimistic typically, even if you're on the correct path for you. If you aren't positive if you are doing the correct factor, try asking somebody you trust, such as a detailed friend or friend.

Clean and organize your personal space. You might be stunned by what quantity your atmosphere affects your mood. Color, for instance, can have a massive result on however individuals feel. Make positive your house is clean and well organized. Paint the walls a different color if you do not like them. Decorate with a design that evokes you and provokes a "beauty response." Have pictures of your darling ones around. Doing these simple home organization techniques can include modification; however, you feel and build it easier to access your true want. Clutter and a poor atmosphere will cause litter in your mind, which can limit your ability to follow your heart.

Part 3: Acting on Your Desire

Engage in communicatory activities. There is a range of inventive activities you'll do to urge connected together with your heart. The goal here is to open yourself to your heart or your innermost desire. Styles of style, like those employed in art medical care, will assist you in becoming a lot more receptive to yourself and your heart. Here are a few ideas for belongings you will do:

**Music -** Try connection a choir or taking stringed instrument lessons.

**Art -** Take a painting class or learn, however, to sculpt.

**Dance -** Enroll in a condiment category or maybe exercise-dancing categories at the athletic facility.

**Drama -** See if there are any open theater teams around you that you will be a part of. Acting is a good way to precise your creativity.

**Free-Write -** Life can cause your true needs and your daily routines to get crusty over with obligations and expectations. A practice like free writing will facilitate you access your heart and start to develop a more in-depth relationship with this essential part of yourself.

Choose a topic and write it at the highest of a chunk of paper. The topic will be one word, like "travel," or it can be a brief statement, like "what I think regarding traveling." Set a timer for 5 or ten minutes and take a look at to jot down regarding the subject while not putting a lot of thought into what you are doing. Don't set up ahead of time. The goal is to let your unconscious mind take over for you instead of letting the center a part of your brain holds the reins.

**Practice Attentiveness -** There are 2 totally different ways that you'll live your life: being and doing. The "doing" mode is what many individuals notice themselves stuck in a very ton of the time. It's a necessary mode for our fast-paced, high-stress culture, and it's actually terribly helpful for keeping up. However, the "doing" mode can build it onerous to listen to your wants and curtail enough to get pleasure from life. Mindfulness meditation will facilitate you strengthen the "being" mode of your life, which is the mode that may assist you to begin to follow your heart.

Sit in a comfortable, upright position. Get used to this position for a number of minutes. Begin to pay attention to what is going on in your experience. You will have a lot of stray thoughts, body sensations, and seemingly random emotional surges. Pay attention to all or any of those things and the rest that happens, doing your best to require a "curious" stance toward them, where you do not get to react to them. Pretend you are someone and you would like to watch this expertise while not intervening. Once you've done this in a safe, quiet, sitting environment, you can attempt it in your way of life, whereas you are doing alternative things.

**Make a Massive Move -** Based on your bucket list and overall life goals, decide to make an enormous move if necessary. This could be going back to high school for a lot of education, moving to another city with higher opportunities or family within sight, or quitting your job to do something that resonates a lot of closely together with your heart's want. It may be an honest plan to speak to your friends and family regarding the move before you begin shifting gears, to see what they think and enlist their support.

**Make Little Changes -** You don't essentially need to build massive changes to alter your life and start to follow your heart. See if there are very little things you will waste your daily routine to feel a lot of attuned to yourself, and you want. For instance, you may wish to pay longer together with your friends or spend less time in front of the TV. Consult your bucket list to see if there are minor changes; you'll build on your life so as to attain what you actually wish out of it.

Understand That Perfection is Fool's Gold

Name one person you know the World Health Organization is flawless by all standards and definitions. (Don't say, God. God is not a person)

A simple google search provides the subsequent definition of the word perfect: "having all the required or fascinating parts, qualities or characteristics." The word "desirable" is the key to know our futile obsession with perfection. Desires are never-ending. As soon as one wants is happy, a new one comes knocking at the door. Perfection or flawlessness is the desired state.

And the interesting factor is, it always remains the desired state. It never becomes a reality. Here is an example: Tom, who makes $20,000 a year, thinks "my financial scenario would be good if I build $50,000 a year". Fast forward five years and Tom is currently creating $50,000 a year. That's his perfect money scenario. Yet currently, Tom feels "my money scenario would be good if I was creating $100,000 a year". The definition of his "perfect financial situation" changes once he gets there.

We will solely pursue perfection and perfection. We will ne'er deliver the goods it as a result of it doesn't extremely exist. It is just like the carrot tied ahead of the donkey and also the donkey eternally chasing it. It can never reach the carrot as a result of once the donkey moves, and the carrot moves with it. We are like the donkey, and also, the state of perfection is that the carrot.

Understanding the Nature of Flaws

We were created with flaws. We all have some gaps in ourselves that we have a tendency to attempt to fill throughout our lives. This is the thrust of existence — the journey from being this to becoming that. Stephen Hawkings, the great uranologist puts it in perspective: "One of the basic rules of the universe is that nothing is ideal. Perfection simply doesn't exist…. Without the state, neither you nor I would exist" —Stephen Hawking.

We are not turning into better when we have a tendency to are an effort to alter by mending our flaws. Rather, we are simply dynamical in our state of existence from being this to being that. This process of becoming or evolving or changing is life. Life is a journey from being flawed to becoming perfect. Imperfection to perfection. This continuous process of becoming is the cloth of all existence. Everything is evolving, changing, becoming one thing alternative than what it's — every moment. You are no exception to that.

Don't Take the Game Too Seriously

Flaws are OK. Flaws are smart. We exist because of our flaws. Don't you see, that's the entire game. This chase for perfection or flawlessness is our life force.

The problem starts once we take this game too seriously. We become all serious and tense up in our pursuit of removing all our "flaws."

Is it wrong to try and take away my flaws? Is it wrong to attempt for perfection? No. There is nothing wrong with needing to remove your flaws. It goes wrong when you become too finite and high regarding this game. When you forget that in the end, this is just a game, a play. It goes wrong when you start hating your flaws with a burning passion. When your flaws build, you grit your teeth and clench your fists. The answer is to first all settle for your flaws. Don't be bitter. Once you do that, life is no longer a struggle. It ceases to be a struggle and becomes fun. From flaw to flawless. One flaw at a time. Enjoy the game.

"Flaw" Is Just a thought. A "flaw" is just an idea. In reality, there is no such thing as a flaw. Blindness is not a flaw in a very country of blind individuals. You are

5ft8inches tall. You want to be 6ft tall. So, your height is a flaw consistent with you. For someone World Health Organization is 5ft3inches tall, your height is perfect. It is not a flaw for that person.

Your flaw is someone else's perfection. Here is another powerful idea: "Your flaws exist only in the lightweight of the existence of others."

If you were the only living human within the world, you would not have any concept of flaws in yourself. Nobody to compare yourself with. Hence no flaws.

Everything Is Perfect because it Is

You have two selections. You can settle for your flaws, and change them, playing on and enjoying the journey. Or you can cry and complain regarding it all you would like. When you settle for your flaws as a district of you, they cease to be flawed. They are there; however, they don't hassle you any longer.

Accepting yourself doesn't mean acceptive solely the smart and positive aspects. It means acceptive your flaws and negative aspects too. Aside regarding yourself becomes a "flaw" once you prefer to see it united. And that choice can greatly impact; however, you read yourself. Accepting your flaws can enable you to settle for yourself absolutely. And that will empower you on the far side of your wildest dreams. Self-acceptance is power.

Say a certain quality in yourself that you see as a flaw, is bothering you too much, then raise yourself this question: am I able to do one thing to alter it? If affirmative, then go ahead and alter it. If no, then learn to accept it wholeheartedly as a district of yourself. What's more? Once you learn to accept your own flaws, you become more acceptive of others and their flaws too. You become less judgmental. And that sets you free on numerous levels. You become more relaxed. Less rigid. Slowly, you come to the realization that there are not any flaws, no mistakes in existence. Everything in existence is ideal, even when it doesn't seem that way.

So, at the end of the day, your flaws don't even matter. Stop losing sleep over your so-called flaws. Accept yourself as you are and permit yourself to feel powerful. Set yourself free from these limiting notions of being flawed or imperfect. They do you no good. And they waste some time and energy. Just perceive this: "There are no mistakes existing. Everything is perfect because it is." At the end of the day, you are the best person for yourself; no one else is as aware of your needs and wants as yourself.

## Chapter 10: How To Develop A Winning

## Mentality

You are required to have a grown mindset for making your life as great as you want. The prime key to achieving all the success that you want in your life is to adopt a winning mentality. Remember, the attitude that you carry forward with yourself plays a great role in determining your success rate. When you say that yes I will win in this, it is very easy to say so but really hard to do it in the right way. You have uttered such words surely for once in your life. No one in this world comes with the desire to lose naturally, but when you figure out that winning actually requires something more from you, you will be setting up a different kind of view for the same.

There are only a few in this world for whom winning has turned out to be a habit. Such people not only achieve what

112

they want to, but they also do the same in a consistent way. The desire and will power of such people is so very strong that it is the only thing that actually helps in waking them up from sleep every morning. It is what makes them give it all they have while working for something which is really important for them. Such people are the ones whom we attribute by using the term gifted or really talented.

It is actually a very easy job to find out various reasons why other people come with the capability of winning and why we are failing constantly. Whenever we come across a winner, we are most likely to get caught in various vague words such as training, talent, and also circumstances as there are various reasons why you are not actually capable of winning the race. "He comes with a great build which provides him with the advantage," "They have the best facilities," "They have a great infrastructure," and various other statements are often made by us in various situations, and many a time, we also use them unconsciously. But, in actual, there is something more to the basic form of winning, something which actually accounts for the consistent form of success. The primary key for becoming a person who makes it a normal course to win every day is to adopt a winner's mentality, a mentality that all those people who achieve greatness maintain in a consistent manner.

Our body comes along with various limitations, but our mind does not. When you want to win something, you are needed to be mentally prepared for the same. You are required to have the mentality which will actually allow you to succeed in the game. This form of mentality is often referred to as the winning mentality. But, how can you define the concept of winning mentality? It is the mentality which you allow you to dig deep in the situation and do all which it takes in relation to putting the efforts, taking action, perseverance and also for inspiring others who are around you for the sole purpose of overcoming any kind of adversity which might come up in the way and will win at the end. It is like willing to do what others are afraid of doing consistently for gaining an advantage of competitive nature and also for mastering the craft for becoming the winner.

Such a form of mentality needs to come from your within, and it is not at all something which can be forced by anyone on you. Someone can tell you repeatedly for developing a winning mentality so that you can win the game, but if you do not have the urge by yourself to win, then no matter what others say, you will never be able to win. The winning mentality can be used in various aspects of life. Whether it is your professional field or any relationship of your life, it can help in all the aspects of life. In case you do not have this kind of mentality, it is possible for you to develop the same over time. So, do you have a winning mentality? Let's have a look at some of the traits which can easily depict if you have the winning mentality or not.

**People with winning mentality pursue improvement relentlessly:** Those who are the winners know it very well that they won't be able to reach where they want to be staying in the same position, and all that they need is a constant improvement. For the purpose of winning, they know that they need to get better every day. It is not actually about any kind of competition; it is mainly about being your best, which you can be. The only thing which can limit the distance that you can go is only your mind. The winners have the habit of breaking the barriers relentlessly which prevents them from improving. They actually try to do what makes them feel uncomfortable in order to grow behind their zone of comfort. It is the only way in which you can turn out to be better than before and win ultimately.

**They find a way for turning adversity into the fuel required for winning:** Adversity affects each and every human being around us. But, in place of just feeling guilty or sorry for themselves, instead of just putting all the blame on someone else or instead of just giving up, the winners know it very well that the only person who can turn them into winners and also change all the circumstances is only themselves. The winners do not have the habit of swimming in the deep pool of self-pity. They know it very well how to pick themselves up as they fail and how to continue with the journey. The winners choose not to actually shift all the blame on others and also accept all the responsibility for carrying the same on their own shoulders. Adversity, along with a bit of change in the opinion, can change into a great form of fuel, which will help in bringing about success.

**They know that luck does not exist in reality:** Luck is nothing but the meeting of preparation with opportunity. When you actually believe in luck, you will start to believe that anything bad or good that you will be getting in your life is all up to chance. The true form of winners leaves nothing for the chance. Each and every one of us gets some kind of opportunity at a particular point in life, but when we are not actually prepared for it, we are most likely to waste it. Some individuals are always prepared and also win when they get their opportunities. The true form of winners actually tries to take it one step further; they try to create their very own opportunities with the help of sheer will power along with all the effort for making sure that they make the best out of what they have.

**They do not love to give up:** The winners do not actually give up in any aspect of their life. When you actually give up, you are never going to win the battle. If you want to make your chances of winning consistently in nature, you are required to master the very art of successful failing. Winning can only be achieved after various attempts, which might also end up in failure and it is known to all the winners.

The 3 C's related to winning mentality

Winning mentality comes along with various factors that can actually help you in winning the race. There are 3 C's which can help in attaining the winning mentality.

**Competitiveness:** Winning is not actually everything, but your will of winning is actually what matters the most. In case you want to succeed in any arena of your life, you are required to want it in the true sense, have the capability of setting it as up an ambitious form of the goal and also have the grunt for working in order to reach your goal. When you turn out to have a mindset of competitive nature, you will find none of the obstacles as being too big for you, which you cannot overcome, no form of a challenge as really a challenge and no pain in the journey which cannot push you through. When you really want to win, you need to have that hunger in yourself which won't allow you to sleep peacefully. You need to have competitive thoughts, always running your mind. No matter what happens, just stick to it. Even if you fail numerous times, you will still be a winner to yourself as you know you have it all that you have.

**Confidence:** The winners come with a silent form of confidence, which will occasionally provide them with enough self-belief which will actually be allowing them to perform at the highest possible level. Such a form of confidence can be attained from a disciplined form of practice, which helps in improving all the skills to a very high level along with quieting all those voices which doubt you and tell you that you can never win. When you are confident enough, you will never have the thought of getting lost. You will be persisting with the belief that the best is still to come which can only be tested at the end. Failing to have enough confidence in yourself, along with all your skills, can actually prevent you from reaching your goal. So, it is really important to level up your confidence right before you prepare to enter the game of reaching your goal. Lack of confidence will surely lead you to failure.

**Composure:** Being composed of your own ability is important when you really want to win. Listening to the outside voices and feeling under-confident with your own abilities won't help. Try to be consistent with what you actually do and what your abilities are. It might happen that at times, your emotions will control your mind and prevent you from performing your best. At such moments, all that you are needed to do is to stay composed with yourself and focus only on the thing which you want to achieve.

How to develop a winning attitude?

You can also develop a winning attitude by following certain techniques. Let's have a look at them.

**Focusing on the passions:** Give yourself enough confidence only by focusing on those things which you love the most. It is much easy to develop a great form of attitude as you delve into doing something which you love. In case you are not at all sure about what you love the most, try to look into your daily habits. You will surely find out all those things which attract you the most and which you love to do.

**Thinking positively:** Start with small things and try to feel positive with even the smallest things that you do. Repeat what you have been doing, and you will be able to develop a positive attitude for it. Think that have you been successful every time in your life? If yes, then why are you allowing the negative things to prevent you from giving your best as you that you will surely succeed? Try to figure out the very reason behind your thoughts. It will actually work and will help you in developing a positive attitude towards your efforts.

**Slowing down the speed of emotions:** When you find yourself thinking in a negative way, try to take a deep breath. You are required to practice mindfulness regularly for calming all your senses. You can control all your racing thoughts when you practice mindfulness regularly, and you will find out that your automatic way of thinking will be coming under your control. It is most likely because our emotions stop us from sensing our surroundings. When you can actually learn to sense your surroundings, you will be able to develop a winning mentality as it helps our minds in gaining positive powers.

**Setting up your goals high and monitoring the progress:** When you try to be realistic, it is not going to change anything. But, when you try to be unrealistic, it will actually help. Setting up goals that are much higher than your imagination can help you in setting up the will power which you need for achieving your limits. Try to enjoy the whole journey and also monitor your progress. Do not just focus on the end results as it will prevent you from achieving your limits. Try getting into the process and move out of the boundary of the outcome.

**Commitment:** When you set up higher goals for yourself, it will be of no help unless and until you can commit to the same to the fullest. If you cannot commit to work towards the goal and achieve the same, you will lack the confidence that you need for your achievement. Commitment is something that can even help you in climbing up a mountain. You might also require to sacrifice various things in your life when you try to commit to achieving something. Remember, when you commit with your will, you will surely succeed.

**Being true to yourself:** You are required to understand that winners actually quit. Those who are winners know exactly where to quit. You need to be true to yourself. In case you have winded up yourself in something which is not your passion in actual, try to be true to your inner-self and move away from it right away. You can look out for something else. It is your own life, and you have all the right to control it. Being fake to yourself will only be harming you. Try to be true and judge the situations in their real sense.

**No excuses:** When you try to make excuses for not doing something or for not being able to do something, it is most likely to turn into a habit. You will be the prime victim of your very own vibrations. You are the one who is actually accountable for your actions and what happens to you. Learn to accept them and own them. When you try to ignore something by making vague excuses, you are actually instilling negativity in your own mind.

Each and every one of us is born with some potential of our own. We all come with something which will allow us to be the winners in our own life. All that you need to do is to just tap your inner potential and try to bring out your winning mentality.

## Chapter 11: Psychological Effects Of

## Worrying

Worry about something or someone is natural. It makes you aware of the consequences of whatever you want to do or think of doing. When you worry only when you are supposed to, it keeps you on alert. The same cannot be said about all worrying. When you worry without cause or reason, it tends to be very harmful to you and anyone around you. Worrying comes from stress and anxiety, and if you let that cloud your mind, there is no way you are going to get things done. Here are some of the psychological effects of worrying.

1. You'll always have negative thoughts:

This particular effect happens to a lot of people with the problem of excessive worry. When you are stressed and anxious all the time, you tend to worry excessively, and when you do, there is a big possibility that you will not be able to see any good scenario for the rest of your life. Some people see the good in anything that is happening now or will happen later, but others will only see the bad in those things. It is not as if they are bad for doing that; it just because their brains have been hot-wired to see only the wrong things because of their excessive worry. For instance, if two people are watching a TV show that features rollercoasters and people riding them and one of those two people worries a lot and the other doesn't, the one that does not worry would be like "Oh this looks like so much fun, I can't wait to get on one of these." While the one that constantly worries would be like, "hat if the railing comes off and everyone falls to their death, no I am never getting on one of these." These are the kind of thoughts that enter the minds of people that have nothing else to do in the world but to worry. These kinds of people experience what is referred to as automatic negative thoughts, meaning that if they are on their own doing absolutely nothing and you walk up to them and tell them about any scenario at all, they must bring out the negative side in it.

2. It could cause addiction:

By now, we all know that worrying all the time can cause more harm than good. Worrying is one of the reasons why we have addicts today. How? Most people that worry a lot tend to use alcohol or drugs to subside their worries, and because they worry all the time, they take more and more with each passing day, and before you know what is going on, they might have taken so many drugs that that could kill them. If you are one of those people that think excessive worry is right, know that there is a possibility that you might end up as an addict. There are also some cases of people overdosing on their stress and anxiety pills. When they notice that their worry is getting the best of them, maybe because of their stress, they tend to take more pills than they're supposed to because they want the effect of the drugs to work faster and to relieve them of their stress almost immediately. This is the reason why stress and anxiety patients are not given their medications to take by themselves when they are in the hospital. The nurse or doctor normally brings the drugs to the patient's room at a designated time to avoid an overdose.

3. Frequent nightmares:

Worrying almost always comes with nightmares. Most times, these nightmares come as a result of the fact that they are unable to do anything but worry. When you continuously have certain things in your mind that cause unnecessary worry, your subconscious mind manifests those fears into nightmares. Those nightmares sometimes make you see what is on your mind in the worst possible scenario. Nightmares can be one of the terrifying things you will face when you worry.

When you have a lot of nightmares, it makes sleeping hard because you will not want to go back to bed when you know that you are just going to see your fears getting played back to you in the worst ways possible. When you have these nightmares, it may occur over and over again. You can only stop these nightmares from reoccurring when you worry less. If you feel like it is not going to be easy, you could get a psychologist to help you with it.

4. Unexpected mood swings:

There are a lot of people that have a lot of sudden mood swings. Sometimes it may be because they are going through a particular stage in their lives, but other times it's because they have things on their minds and things that get them stressed and worried. There are cases where a person is happy now, and two minutes later, the person becomes sad and or depressed. This is because they probably remembered something that makes them worry or something that makes them unnecessarily uneasy. When you see people like this, you must get them some help as soon as possible. Just imagine not being able to understand how someone feels simply because their mood swings are out of this world. This can even make them lose friends because not a lot of people have the time and energy to tolerate their mood swings. Some friends may stay with you through that tough time, probably because they've been with you all your life, but the ones that have not been with you for a long time will run away from you as fast as they got into your life.

With all of the bad effects of worrying, some people will still think that worry benefits people in so many ways. You can still think like that if you want. Just get ready to be addicted to one substance or the other all in the name of being overworried about something or someone.

Can Worry Affect Your Physical Health?

This is a question that everyone asks, but no one answers. There are a lot of physical challenges that come with worrying excessively. When you tend to worry a lot and are on edge all the time because you think something terrible is going to happen to you at any moment, you are bound to face some particular physical challenges when it comes to your health. You can try to hide them because you probably believe in one worry myth, but with time, you will not be able to do so anymore because it will be out in the open. This problem occurs most times when fight or flight is triggered by excessive worry and anxiety. They cause the body's sympathetic nervous system to release stress hormones like cortisol.

The hormones released by these triggers can help you in different ways, but they are also harmful to the body to a certain extent. They could cause a series of physical challenges that will not be in your best interest at all. Some of these challenges include headaches, inability to concentrate, irritability, muscle aches, muscle tension, nausea, nervous energy, rapid breathing, shortness of breath, sweating, trembling and twitching, difficulty swallowing, dizziness, dry mouth, fast heartbeat, and fatigue.

If the excessive fuel in your bloodstream is not used for physical activities, it may be harmful to you in so many ways. Some of which include suppression of the immune system, digestive disorders, muscle tension, short-term memory loss, premature coronary artery disease, and heart attack. These and many more can happen to you when you overworry. You may think that worrying is not as bad as people say, but it is. Imagine getting short-term memory loss when you are not old at all. How will you be able to get on with your life when your life has all of these? If you want to worry constantly, you should try and worry about what could happen to you when you worry because it is essential, and it could end your life. If you have excessive worry and anxiety, it may be terrible for an individual, especially if that worry and anxiety go untreated. When you notice that you worry a lot, you must let someone know as soon as possible because if you don't, it may lead to depression and in worse cases, suicidal thoughts.

Stress is simply a trigger for worry; it could be bad or good for you, depending on how you tend to handle it.

How to Help Excessive Worriers

If you want to stop worrying so much, there are some things that you should try to help you worry less. You will need to change your lifestyle to understand how your worry works and how you can reduce or completely get rid of it. Before starting any of this, it's imperative to know that you will not get any good results if you do not want it in the first place.

1. Daily exercises:

This is one of the best ways to reduce stress and worry. Exercise helps the body in so many ways, but when it comes to worrying, it reduces the chemicals that may cause unnecessary challenges through physical activities. Those chemicals are now spread into different places in the body, meaning that you are burning them out little by little. Before doing any exercise, it is imperative that you let your doctor know first if you have any medical issues. Sometimes, doctors can tell you the kind of exercises that would suit you better, and the kind of exercises that will make you get what you want faster. Sometimes, your doctor may have certain exercise groups that they will want you to try. These groups may have people with your condition, and when you exercise with people that are like you, it motivates you to want to be better, and it also makes you want to do more and finally accomplish what you are looking for. For some people that do not want crowds and a lot of people around them, you could get a personal trainer recommended by the doctor. The only downside to this is that you are going to be spending more.

2. Visit a doctor:

This is something that everyone should do even before exercising. You need to see a doctor that you trust, that will understand you, and help you with anything that you might need. When you are done talking with him or her, get some physical examinations done to make sure that there is nothing adding to your anxiety and worry. You may think that you have just one problem, not knowing that there are a lot more problems for you to tackle before getting what you want, which is a worry-free life. After the examination, if the doctor notices that it's just anxiety and depression, the doctor may choose to give you certain drugs that will help you reduce them. These drugs may be antidepressants or anti-anxiety medications. After taking the drugs from the doctor, you mustn't overdose because you think the worry is getting worse. There are a lot of stories of people overdosing on antidepressants because the worry and stress were getting unbearable. When you notice that you are getting more worried, all you have to do is to go back to the hospital, see the doctor again and he will know what to do. Some doctors get the patient professional help by referring them to certain specialists that will help them work on their anxiety and stress without overdosing. If you must take more than your prescription, the least you can do before doing that is to consult your doctor first, and then you will know what to do.

3. Always eat healthily:

Eating healthily is something that will help you a lot, especially when you worry. Some people eat less when they are worried, and some eat a lot more when they are worried. These two cases can cause some severe defects that could be extremely harmful to the human body. Others switch from the healthy food they are used to eating and start eating unhealthy foods that will only make them feel worse than they already are. When you overeat and worry at the same time, you may not see yourself getting obese, and that comes with a whole lot of challenges, and you don't want obesity to add to your already constant worrying streak. When you notice that you are eating more than usual when you are stressed or depressed, learn to practice some restraint. When you hold back any time you want to eat more, it will tell your body that you are not giving in and with time, you will notice that it will be easier to handle your stress. If you are the type that does not eat enough during stress, you need to start eating. It doesn't mean that you should eat till you drop, all you have to do is to eat healthy and controlled portions. All this is very easy to say but somewhat difficult to accomplish. When you know what you want and what you need to get it, you will remain the focus. If you still think you cannot do this alone, you could get some help from your friends, family members, or a trained psychologist. You should note that things like these are not supposed to be kept to oneself. It is something that should not be done alone.

4. Reduce your caffeine intake:

This method may not go down well with a lot of people that are already used to drinking a lot of coffee. Some people cannot do without having caffeine for a day. If you are one of those people, you need to control your caffeine intake. This doesn't mean that you should stop drinking coffee all at once. If you were used to drinking coffee three times a day, you could slowly reduce it to two and then to one cup a day. The reason why you should do it slowly is that if you quit all at once, your body may not handle the rejection very well. Caffeine only makes you jumpy and more agitated. When you have anxiety and worry problems, caffeine is not the way to go because it can take sleep away from you, which will make you more vulnerable to any and everything that your worry had to throw at you. You may think that you cannot do without drinking coffee, but if you think about it, how did you use to manage when you had no coffee in your life? This is a question you should ask yourself before using the words "I cannot do without it."

5. Learn to be aware of your worries:

This is something that every worrier should learn. You need to know when your worry is about to take over you. When you do, it will be easier for you to take control of it. Some people put specific triggers on their bodies to help them get over the stress when it is about to take over them. Some people put rubber bands on their wrist and consistently hit themselves with it anytime their worry is about to take over them. You can use any trigger you want if you think the rubber band is going to be painful. The reason why the rubber band trigger is more popular is that it is one of the most effective. When you know that you are going to feel some pain any time you want to get into your depressed state, you are going to have a big rethink of what you are about to do. You need to understand that your worries come from you and you alone, which means that you are the only one that can get rid of them.

You can set out some time each day to reflect on your worries and fears. You do not have to set out a whole day for reflecting on your fears because that would be wrong. You can set out 10 to 15 minutes a day to reflect on what your concerns are and how you can get over them. When you are done with that, you can sit down and tell yourself that you are going to let go of those fears and worries immediately that the stipulated time is over. When you learn how to think of things and let go of them the moment you are done worrying about them, there will be no need for you to go through stress. If you have a lot of worries, you mustn't reflect on all of them on the same day because when you do, you tend to spend more time on the worries which you don't want. For instance, you can set your mind to tackle about two fears today for that particular stipulated time. When you are done with that, you can always try and get rid of the rest the next day and other days after that.

5. Try as much as possible to relax:

Relaxation is something that every worrier needs. When you worry all the time, you need to relax and think about nothing but your health. If you do not feel relaxed in the environment you find yourself in, you could go somewhere else or even go on a vacation. You can take a leave or something because you will not be able to work correctly when your head is somewhere else. You can take strolls or go to tranquil places with beautiful views where you can think about the things that are there. You should only think of the things that are right in front of you at that moment; it helps you forget about your worries or the past. You must take people that make you feel safe and relaxed. When you are around people who want the best for you, it speeds up your healing process. If you don't have anyone like that, you can go by yourself but make sure that you try as much as possible to reflect on the now because it is one of the most important things you need to do when you get to wherever you are going to for relaxation.

The benefits of relaxation when it comes to worrying are just uncanny because it helps improve stress management and also helps to reduce depression, which means that you will be getting a lot of benefits only by sitting or lying in a quiet place doing nothing. This is one of the easiest ways to get rid of your anxiety and worry for good. Some common relaxation techniques could also help, and they include deep abdominal breathing, meditation, listening to calming music, and other activities like yoga and tai chi. There are a lot of ways to relax; find the one that suits you.

6. Create a strong social network background:

When you feel lonely and isolated, it will make it harder for you to manage your stress. If you are the type that does not have a lot of friends, you can make friends to make sure that you are not lonely. You must not make just friends. Get closer to your family members, attend a gathering, go out, and take your mind off certain things. When you do, it will be easier for you to get rid of your worries. When you are always cooped up in your house or your room doing nothing, your worries will keep coming, and you will not be able to do anything about them. Learn to be social; you could even open a social media account to help you meet friends faster and more conveniently. Statistics show that people who are happily married or have good social relationships find get sick less easily and have less serious chronic illness. This is because they are always active with friends, family, or both. This is one of the best ways to get rid of your worries. Get together with friends and make some memorable moments that you will remember for the rest of your life. Let those memories take over your worries and fears. When you put your mind to the things you can accomplish in the now and forget what the world has done to you, it will help you worry a lot less.

Most times, we are the cause of our own problems. We are the ones that decide to get stressed and overworried when we have been told not to and even after getting the remedies for our stress, we refuse to follow them for reasons best known to us. You should know by now that worrying could be fatal. There are a lot of people that get extremely worried about something and die because they did not have help when they were depressed. Even after some people get remedies and help from professionals, it is still a huge struggle to get them out of it.

## Chapter 12: How To Quit Worrying,

## Anxiety And Negative Emotions

You have identified that you are an over-thinker so what can you do about it?

Unfortunately there is no switch in your brain that you can just click on and off whenever you feel like it but there are a variety of techniques you can use to reduce or even eliminate overthinking which hopefully will, in turn, reduce your anxiety. These aren't quick fixes however and may take some practice before you start to notice a difference.

Start making small decisions and go with your gut

When my friend texts me to ask where I want to go for lunch I don't have to look at every single café, pub and restaurant. We are staying in the local area so we know all the good places. All I have to decide is whether I want to drive and how far and what I feel like eating. To reduce my overthinking I stopped second guessing myself. I told myself that my friend had asked what I would like to do and therefore I wouldn't worry about her. If she had a particular place in mind then she would have just suggested it.

By starting to make these small decisions quickly I started to realize there weren't any devastating consequences to it; yes, occasionally I chose a place that had slow service or the food wasn't very good but so what? Nothing catastrophic happened, my friend is still my friend. Eventually it became easier to make bigger decisions as well without stressing about it afterwards.

Limit Choices

The Internet can be an over-thinker's nightmare. The world we live in today means we have so many choices, which can make it nigh on impossible to make a decision when you struggle to do this anyway.

However, you DON'T have to look at every variation of a single item. For example, if you need a gift for somebody you don't need to look at a million products as well as their reviews on a hundred different websites. Instead try to choose a gift that you want to get them, decide whether you want to purchase online or in a store and then just search for two or three different ones and look at the reviews.

Look At the Bigger Picture

Over-thinkers have a tendency to focus on and worry about everything from money and bills to whether people are talking about them behind their backs or whether they've embarrassed themselves in a certain situation. To the person thinking these thoughts they are major concerns yet are they really?

When you find yourself overthinking something, pause, take a deep breath and ask yourself; "will this matter to me in three years, three months, three weeks or even three days?" Chances are it won't.

Distinguish between the small decisions that don't have any consequences other than maybe mild embarrassment such as picking a bad restaurant to those that may have bigger consequences such as maybe painting your walls a terrible color to those that could have even bigger consequences like failing an exam. Then look at the outcomes realistically. Let's be honest, rarely anything has life-changing consequences; so you pick a bad restaurant, okay you're embarrassed, your friends might tease you but so what? Nobody else is thinking about it except you. Okay, you paint your walls a terrible color? So what, you can repaint them eventually. Okay, you fail an exam? So what, you can probably re-sit it or make your grade up by doing better in the next set of assignments or exams. Once you look at the bigger picture you realize that it isn't worth the worry.

Stop striving for perfection. Sadly life isn't perfect and neither are we as humans. Always strive to give one hundred percent in whatever you do and always aim to do your best but if things don't go your way, as long as what you have done is 'good enough' then be proud.

Learn From Your Mistakes

If you feel you handled a situation wrong you may constantly go over and over in your head how you could have done it better but at the end of the day you cannot go back in time and change it. You will have to deal with the consequences regardless of whether you spend five minutes or five days thinking about it. Rather than beat yourself up about it, think about what you could have done differently should you end up in a similar situation and then move on.  It may sound scary but really what is the alternative; is it better to make a wrong decision than never make any decision or never put forward an opinion just in case somebody disagrees with you?

Make Your Overthinking Productive

I have said previously that overthinking doesn't get us anywhere because we spend so much time thinking and worrying about our actions that we don't really do anything.

However worry can motivate you into taking action if we use it to our advantage and this is where we can distinguish between productive and unproductive worry.

Imagine you have an exam. You find you are sat on the sofa thinking about it constantly, you feel sick and you can't stop thinking what if you fail or what if you can't answer any questions. These thoughts make you spring into action; you make a study timetable, you stick up post its around the house with key information on, you make a list of the topics you are not sure of and revise these first, you ask somebody to quiz you and take mock tests. When you go into your exam, you may still be worrying but you know you have done everything you could possibly do to prepare. This is productive worrying;

thinking about an issue and taking steps to resolve it.

Using the example above, unproductive worry would be continuing to sit on the sofa and think about how unprepared you are, how much you hate exams, you are going to fail, you are not smart enough, you don't know anything and so on. This fear of failure paralyzes you and you end up not doing anything. You go into your exam unprepared and you continue to think these negative thoughts during the exam. This is unproductive worry; you focused on the issue but you didn't do anything about it.

Clearly unproductive worry is just a waste of time so when you find yourself thinking about something start taking action to resolve the situation rather than burying your head in the sand.

Put Time Aside To Worry

Rather than while away your hours just constantly thinking about 'what ifs', schedule a time in your day to worry and put a time limit on it. This may sound a bit silly but actually it is sensible to think as long as it is productive. This may be twenty minutes in a morning or after work. If you commute to work on public transport then this maybe a good time to do this. For others it helps to have their worry time a couple of hours before bed, this gives them time to get it out of their head and unwind before trying to sleep.

The trick to this is to not set too high a time limit too. If it's that you are thinking about what you may have done the night before when you were out in a bar with your friends then tell yourself firmly "I will think about this at (whatever time you decide works for you) for twenty minutes". This is usually an issue that as the day goes on becomes less of an issue if you are not thinking about it. It doesn't warrant hours and hours on it. If you are overthinking about a gift idea for someone then you may want a bit longer as this will give you time to start searching for ideas on the internet.

Whatever time limit you set be strict with yourself. Once it's finished, get up, put it out of your mind and find something different to do.

Write It Down

My son was diagnosed with an anxiety disorder and it was suggested that he write down his fears and put them inside a worry monster. If you haven't seen these, they are little soft toys with wide open mouths; the child writes on a piece of paper what they are worried about and then they push them inside the mouth. The monster then 'eats' these whilst the child sleeps. The idea is that once the worries are on paper the child can push them out of their mind.

It does seem to work and whilst as an adult you might not want a worry monster, the theory of writing your thoughts down so you don't have to think them anymore is still valid.

Now be careful; making hundreds of to do lists ISN'T helpful BUT having a pen and notepad handy for your scheduled 'thinking time' can be. Rather than going around in circles repeating the same thought in your head, simply write down what is bothering you, what the (realistic) consequences might be and what you can do. This can be in the form of a list, a spider diagram or a table; whatever you find easier.

Once your thinking time is up, put aside your notebook or whatever you have written your worries down on and leave it until the next day or the day after. This can help you see that your concerns weren't anything to worry about and most of the time the issue resolves itself, if not you have a plan of what you can do to spur yourself into taking action.

 "But if I could solve my issues I wouldn't be overthinking them?" You may be great at coming up with consequences but not solutions. If this is the case then write down a person who you could talk to who may be able to help. This could be a colleague or boss if your issue is work related or it could be a friend or relative if your issue is personal. If you can't think of anybody then simply write down "unsure at this time" or something similar. The point of this exercise still stands; write it down and put it out of your mind for a while.

Note that I wrote the words "realistic consequences" and not just "consequences". This is because over-thinkers have a tendency to think about what the worst thing could happen be rather than what will realistically happen. For example, let's say you've gone for a job interview and you don't think you've done very well. You may think about disastrous consequences like, I didn't get the job, I have no money, I'm going to lose my house and end up living on the streets. Is this realistically going to happen in the next week or even month? Chances are you will apply for more jobs and although they might not be as good as this one, you will eventually get one. If you are unemployed at the moment you can usually ring up companies and explain your situation and get an extension on things like your electricity, gas and phone bills, etc. You can ring the bank or landlord and get an extension on your rent. Depending on where you live there might be state help. If you live with someone or have family around they may be able to help out; yes it may be embarrassing to ask but if the alternative truly was living on the streets then asking for help is only sensible. By looking at the realistic consequences and what we can realistically do to solve them can stop these worries becoming huge and unmanageable.

Find a Distraction

Once you notice that you are overthinking it is time to do something else to distract yourself. Some people find switching on the TV, reading or listening to music can help with this. Personally I find that I can completely tune these things out if I am in serious overthinking mode but what doesn't work for one person may work for another so it is always worth a try.

I prefer hobbies that I have put all my concentration and thought into in order to complete such as jigsaw puzzles, knitting, cross stitch or sewing projects, model building and so on. Once you become engrossed in the task at hand you don't have chance to start worrying about that looming deadline or what people have been saying about you at the school gates for a while.

If you find yourself lying in bed going over the same thoughts then STOP THIS! Don't lie in bed for more than fifteen minutes no matter how tired you are. If you find yourself overthinking and know you are not going to get to sleep then get up, no matter how difficult it feels. Go into another room and either write down the thoughts that are in your head or try to read a book. Remember you're not trying to keep yourself awake though so try to keep the lighting dim. Sometimes just this act of moving when we're tired can stop our minds whirring.

Get Physical

As an over-thinker I know that it can be very difficult to break the cycle simply by turning the television on. What does help a lot of people though is doing a physical activity such as running, going to the gym, swimming or yoga and so on. Even just getting out of the house for a fifteen minute walk can help you focus on something more positive. At first you may find you're still thinking but eventually you may find you start to tune into your physical self rather than your mind.

Focus On the Here and Now

Sometimes we can be worrying about the past or stressing about what the future may hold that we don't concentrate on what is happening our lives at this present moment. If you are out with friends force yourself to concentrate and join in with the conversation around you. If you find yourself overthinking at home, switch activities to try to distract you.

Swap the Mental Chatter

When our minds are overactive the more you try not to think the harder it can be to stop. Therefore instead of trying to stop thinking altogether, just switch what is going on in your head. For example, as silly as it sounds, counting sheep when you're trying to get to sleep can help because it stops your overthinking and gives you something different to focus on. Listing prime numbers, counting backwards from a number in twos, threes or fours, going through the times tables, listing countries or names alphabetically are also good ways to tune your brain in to something else.

Some research has been done to see the affects on people who repeat the word 'the' over and over again and it is thought that this kind of repetition does calm down our minds and stop us from overthinking so next time you're having trouble sleeping, choose a random word and repeat it over and over, taking notice of how the letters and sounds change the more you focus on it.

## Chapter 13: Keep Your Brain In Peak

## Condition

8.1  Mind Games

Just as how we keep our body active, we need to invest time to keep our mind active too. The same importance we give to our bodies sometimes is not cascaded down to our brains. While a little bit of reading is great, research shows that varying our mental health activity is the element to long-term peak brain success.

According to findings by Neuroscience, a human brain reaches peak performance between 16 to 25 years old and after this, the cognitive function starts declining.

While it does not sound like such good news, the great thing is no matter how old you are, science proves that with constant and persistent brain exercises, it can benefit your brain.

There are many ways in which you can train your brains such as reading, of course, writing, Sudoku and crossword puzzles, brain teasers and always learning new things and challenging your mind.

Benefits of challenging your mind:

It improves your memory

It improves your logic

It increases your attention and focuses

Your verbal skills improve

According to Dr. Sherry Willis from the University of Texas, brain training enables individuals to become more efficient at performing daily tasks even from the mundane to the more technical ones. Intelligence is not a fixed element in the person that you are. It is not something that you are born with. It depends on your environmental and societal factors, your experiences, the desire to learn more as well as your passion. By keeping your brain on its toes, you can ensure that your brain is exercised properly and to its fullest potential.

## 8.2   Physical Exercises

It is a known fact that regular exercise can protect your health and help you maintain an ideal body weight in the long run. But did you know that it can also yield additional benefits for the busy professional such as yourself? Studies have shown that regular exercise releases hormones to boost your mood, reduce stress, helps you sleep better at night and if performed in the mornings, help jump-start your day. In the end, exercise helps to boost productivity at work and ultimately boost your business success. Here are some examples of how regular exercise can help not only improve your health but your professional career as well:-

Goal Setting And Determination

When we start exercising or picking up a new sport, we will always set goals for us to achieve. The training we put into these goals such as completing a marathon can help business professionals use that same determination and drive to pursue the challenges and objectives they face in the boardroom.

Increase Your Confidence

Every time you hit the gym and accomplish a goal that you set for that workout, you begin to feel good about yourself. This accomplishment by having a great workout can translate into every area in your life. This can improve your confidence level throughout the day and make you feel great about everything you set yourself to do.

Improve Creativity And Thinking Skills

Studies have shown that exercise does not only benefit the physical part of your body but also the mental part as well. It was shown that cardio exercise not only improved the aerobic capacity of an individual but also improved their cognitive functions as well. The increase in blood flow to the brain has shown to be the main cause of this increase.

Reduces Stress

When we are stressed, we notice that we are unable to act and think properly thus we end up making a lot of not-so-good decisions at work. Exercising helps us battle this stress by releasing endorphins when we induce our bodies through physical activities. These endorphins give us a natural high and allow us to approach our day with a calmer mindset.

Increase Energy Levels

Working day in and day out can lead to an increase in fatigue levels to an individual. If you don't fight this, you end up going to work with low energy levels that will inhibit your performance at work. In a study done on the effect of exercise on an individual's energy levels, it was shown that performing exercises on a daily basis helped them to increase their energy levels by 20 percent while it also helped to reduce their fatigue levels by 65 percent.

Exercising regularly not only helps you to be awake throughout the entire day but it has shown through this study that it helps you get better sleep at night. We have gone through some of the important points why exercising is important both physically and mentally to a busy professional like yourself. But if you have not exercised before or had trouble getting into a routine, it can be a daunting task to reap those benefits that we spoke off earlier. So, the best thing we need to do to build a routine out of exercising is to plan ahead. Let's see the steps that we can take:-

Goal Setting

Determine the individual goals that you want to achieve. It can be from reducing your weight or picking up a new sport. Whatever it may be, be sure to note it down and focus on it.

Choosing Your Workout Times

Choose a time in the day that you feel you can focus on and complete your workouts. This can be either early in the day or at night. There can even be a case where you can sneak in an exercise during lunchtime if your office has a gym. But ultimately, you have to decide what is best for you and a routine that you will most likely stick to base on your busy schedule. Another important aspect to remember is to always listen to your body. If your body is still sore from your previous workout, or you are feeling tired sick, best to skip the workout for that day. But don't skip the next one when you feel better.

Choosing An Exercise

Once you have set your goals and workout time, it is no time to choose what workout you want to do. This can be as simple as going for a jog or doing jump ropes. Swimming is another popular exercise that is easy and convenient to do. Joining a local gym and signing up for their aerobic or yoga classes also is a popular choice amongst busy professionals. How about hitting those weights? Don't know where to start? Get a personal trainer to help you through the basic and fundamental movements. The most important criteria to remember here is to select an activity whether it be a solo or a group activity that most likely you would stick to in the long run and become a part of your daily routine.

Learn To Have Fun

The one final thing that you will need to know once you have covered all the other aspects above is to have fun with the exercise you are doing. Ensure that the activity that you have chosen doesn't make you feel bored and not fun. When you keep things energized you less likely to give up. So for this, try to join a class or get a workout partner as a start to push you and keep you occupied.

8.3  Making Time in Your Life

For most of us managing our time becomes such a challenge day by day that it will ultimately affect our productivity. We can't seem to reduce the number of tasks that keep piling on our to-do-list and we just keep getting bombarded with emails, write-ups, reports and not to mention our own personal and household responsibilities.

In 1955, in an essay by Cyril Northcote Parkinson, he coined a phrase known as the "Parkinson Law." He states that "work expands so as to fill the time available for its completion." What this means is that the more time we allocate for completing a task or project, we end up taking more time to complete it. Hence, many at times we feel that we can't complete a task even if we thought we have given ourselves ample time to work on it. In the end, the only way we can negate this is to put stricter deadlines and really push yourself to complete them. That's where the "Pomodoro Technique" comes in to play.

This technique is a time management technique that focuses on grouping tasks into 25 minute windows of time. For each 25 minute time window, you will be allocated a 5-minute break. Once complete four 25 minute windows in succession, you are allowed a longer break which is usually between 15 to 30 minutes. This system was introduced in the late 1980s by a man called Francesco Cirillo.

This system works because instead of focusing on one particular task for an extended period of time, you actually break it down to smaller manageable windows. Also, with the smaller time frame, you will be less tempted to break away and do other unwanted tasks such as checking your email, going through social media or any other distracting activity. Through the Pomodoro Technique, you will find that you end up getting your tasks completed due to this newfound sense of urgency, you will be able to focus on the task at hand, you avoid multi-tasking completely, reduce your stress levels and you will also increase your determination and concentration in completing a task.

Here are some simple steps to get going with the Pomodoro Technique: -

Determine your task and decide how much time you will need to complete it

Using a timer on your mobile phone, set it to 25 minutes.

Focus and work on this specific task for 25 minutes. Resist the urge to be distracted.

While you are trying to accomplish your task, do not try to multitask other random tasks.

Once the 25 minutes are up, take a quick 5-minute break and get back to the task if you haven't completed it or move on to another task if you have completed the previous one.

Remember, once you have completed four Pomodoros in succession, take a 15-30 minute break.

Just like any technique, there are guidelines that you will need to understand and follow in order to maximize your result. Here are four of them: -

Remember to take your breaks – When the timer stops, stop your task. You will need this break to relax and refocus back on your next task. Do a task that takes your mind away from work but won't consume more than the 5-minute window allocated.

Task Time Length – This isn't much of a guideline as it is a variation. Sometimes a given task can take more than 25 minutes. As such, you can combine two Pomodoros and take the combined break time as allocated. But one thing here is not to go beyond three Pomodoros at one time.

Batching Pomodoros – If a specific task takes less than 25 minutes to complete, group several Pomodoros that can be fitted into the 25 minute window time frame.

Using the Pomodoro Technique, you will find yourself being able to easily focus your thoughts and get into the zone in completing a task without being distracted. Many might think this method is too systematic or regimented, but this technique is one sure-fire way to ramp up your productivity and keep yourself focused.

8.4  Designing Your Plan

Deciding what your mission is will set the course of your journey- what you want to achieve by the end of it, where you see yourself at the end of this journey and what you hope to change and what you hope to keep. Consistency and discipline are the one thing that separates an averagely talented person doing something extraordinary and a naturally talented person doing something mediocre with their lives, not using their talents to the fullest potential.

A person's achievement is a contribution of different qualities. Each quality represents a different improvement in a person's life. A person can be super talented, have the right connections, be at the right place at the right time or Lady Luck just happened to be smiling on them at that precise moment. They can have all the right things going on for them in order to achieve success.

The truth is, there is a slight difference between people who are genuinely successful and those that just got their 15 minutes of luck or fame. For long-term and sustainable success and happiness, the one thing that enables all of this is, being DISCIPLINED.

Designing your life mission is something you cannot see or touch or taste or smell but its effects are momentous. It can transform the fat into the slim, poor into rich, depressed to happy. Yes, you can say that luck plays a role but self- discipline, and productivity are what prepares you to face what this lucky break may bring.

If you want to become a highly successful person, then the first step is to define your goals, to find your mission in life. All of us here can become somebody, so become somebody. We are all here for a reason and we all have significance in this world and all of us are given unique attributes.

Some people are lucky to have attributes that are quite obvious like talent in singing and dancing whereas some take time to discover these attributes. Some don't even know they had it in them until they were pushed to their limits or came out of their comfort zone.

Michael Gerber, in his book 'E-Myth: Why Most Small Businesses don't Work' instruct readers to visualize the day of their funeral. When visualizing this, he asks readers to imagine what their eulogy would be like, what would their lifetime achievements be, what would people remember most of them and what would matter most at the end of their lives.

To become disciplined and productive is to also have a purpose in life. What are your goals?

By writing your personal mission statement, it gives you the opportunity to establish what is important to you and it helps you make the necessary decisions to stick to your goals. For some, a mission statement helps them to chart a new course in life.

Think about what outcome you want to see or feel or reap by the end of it. Remember when you create this mission statement, it is your responsibility to stick to it and see this through.

Let's start by doing a little exercise. Get a pen and paper and write down your personal mission statement:

What are the things that are most important to you?

What are the things that you want to do in this life?

What are your values and beliefs?

What are your personal goals?

What are your professional goals?

When doing this exercise, remember that creating your mission statement isn't a one-time thing that's set in stone. Give yourself that opportunity to review your mission statement annually and see if it has resulted in aligning positively with your life, career, jobs, and relationships. Make adjustments if necessary.

Once you are done writing your personal mission statement, you need to think about how you will accomplish this. Let's just say that your mission statement at the end of your productivity journey is to lead a healthier life. Here are some examples of how you can accomplish this:

Wake up early and do a 10-minute exercise

Meal prep for the week so you do not create any cravings to indulge in

Surround yourself with likeminded people

Join a boot camp or fitness class that you are interested in

No matter what your bottom line is, no matter what goals you have- whether it is to climb the corporate ladder, save a certain amount of money, lose weight and get fit or even work on your relationship- all these things can be achieved by practicing productivity. Because not only will you accomplish your goals, you will also lead a healthier lifestyle and above all, be happy. Jesse Owens, American Olympic track gold medallist once said 'We all have dreams. But in order to make dreams come into reality, it takes an awful lot of determination, dedication, self-discipline, and effort'.

At times when there is a conflict or barrier when working on your goals, people with self-control were much better equipped at dealing with these conflicts than those without. People with self-control, a positive mindset, discipline, and higher productivity spend less time indulging with habits or behaviors that distract them from achieving their goals. Here are some traits of productive people:

They are able to make positive decisions much more easily.

They do not make choices based on their feelings or impulses

They make informed, rational decisions

They do not get overly stressed or upset by any changes that come their way

Success isn't something someone is born with. It is cultivated and learned behavior. It requires one to repeat and practice their day-to-day tasks. Now that you know what, why and how- you can begin to piece your mission statement together. A mission statement shouldn't belong either- it should be something that you can sum up in one or two sentences. Write down your mission statement and place it somewhere you can always see is that it can give you motivation when you just aren't feeling like working out or putting in those extra hours. Once you have done your mission statement, it's time to kick start your journey towards being a highly productive individual!

Creating a Personal Commitment

One of the first few things anyone must do to become productive is to make a personal commitment. Your commitment should be that from this day forward, you are going to do the things you know you must do, and when must you do them.

This commitment must include the rule that you cannot allow yourself to make excuses or justify why you aren't doing what you are supposed to be doing. Yes, it's hard to do but the key here is to start small. It's the process, not the end result.

Doing small changes in your daily life will help you towards becoming productive and self-disciplined. Start your day by waking up early. If your regular wake up time is at 8 am, then make it 7.30 am. Make your bed or empty out the trash. All these tiny things are what get you en route to become more disciplined. Robert Collier wisely said 'Success if the sum of small efforts, repeated day in day out'. Becoming disciplined may seem like the hardest thing you can do, but the rewards are immense. A successful life is built on a foundation of the discipline.

Building Your Personal Commitment to Change

## Conclusion

Put a stop to chronic worrying. Worrying is a mental habit you can learn how to break from. Strategies such as creating a worry period, challenging anxious thoughts, and learning to accept uncertainty can help you to significantly reduce worry and calm your anxious thoughts.

Choosing positivity over negativity is the new action plan. Do not be left out on this move. We are seeing the bright side of life henceforth. This is one certified way to live life fully and largely.